RUNNING

A THOUSAND

MILES FOR

FREEDOM

RUNNING

The Escape of

A THOUSAND

William and Ellen Craft

MILES FOR

from Slavery

FREEDOM

by William Craft and Ellen Craft

Introduction by Barbara McCaskill

BROWN THRASHER BOOKS

THE UNIVERSITY OF GEORGIA PRESS

ATHENS AND LONDON

Published in 1999 as a Brown Thrasher Book
by the University of Georgia Press
Athens, Georgia 30602
www.ugapress.org
Introduction © 1999 by the University of Georgia Press
Designed by Erin Kirk New
Set in 11 on 14 Monotype Bulmer by G&S Typesetters

Printed digitally in the United States of America

Library of Congress Cataloging in Publication Data

Craft, William.
Running a thousand miles for freedom : the escape of William and
Ellen Craft from slavery / by William Craft and Ellen Craft ;
introduction by Barbara McCaskill.
xxv, 112 p. : ill. ; 22 cm.
Originally published: London : William Tweedie, 1860.
With supplemental materials.
"Brown Thrasher books."
Includes bibliographical references.
ISBN 0-8203-2104-4 (pbk. : alk. paper)
1. Craft, William. 2. Craft, Ellen. 3. Fugitive slaves — United
States — Biography. 4. Fugitive slaves — England — Biography.
5. Slaves — Georgia — Biography. 6. Slaves' writings, American.
I. Craft, Ellen. II. Title. III. Title: Escape of William and
Ellen Craft from slavery.
E450.C8   1999b
973'.00496073'0922 — dc21
[B]   98-41981

ISBN-13: 978-0-8203-2104-2

British Library Cataloging in Publication Data available

Originally published as *Running a Thousand Miles for Freedom; or,
The Escape of William and Ellen Craft from Slavery*
in 1860 by William Tweedie, London.

CONTENTS

Introduction vii

✠

Running a Thousand Miles for Freedom

✠

INTRODUCTION

William and Ellen Craft
in Transatlantic Literature and Life

Barbara McCaskill

In the literature and lore of transatlantic abolition, *Running a Thousand Miles for Freedom* (1860) is one of the most extraordinary, yet least often evaluated, works. Anthologies more routinely include *The Interesting Narrative of the Life of Olaudah Equiano* (1789), which went into its eighth edition in less than five years, *The Narrative of the Life of Frederick Douglass* (1845), which reached nine British printings in a phenomenal two years, or *Incidents in the Life of a Slave Girl* by Harriet Jacobs (1861), which probably would have gone into several editions if the nation had not plunged into the Civil War.[1]

Frederick Douglass may have been the abolitionists' thunder. Harriet Tubman may have been their fierce, unflappable soldier. The movement's love child, John Brown, may have been the hellbent angel and their homespun mystic and martyr. Without a shred of doubt, however, the Crafts, going by their sobriquet of the "Georgia Fugitives," rivaled the celebrity of all these icons in the decades following their flight from bondage. As Arna Bontemps writes in his *Great Slave Narratives* (1969), an important attempt at identifying the influence, reception, and quality of the genre, "Apparently no two slaves in their flight for freedom ever thrilled the world so much as did this handsome young couple." They "became heroes, about whom speeches were made and poems written" (269).

For all this glory, the Crafts were Georgia's heroes without a home. Peruse any respectable history of African American life and culture—from a university classroom standard like *From Slavery to Freedom* (1997) to a bookstore staple like the three-volume *Afri-*

can Americans: Voices of Triumph (1993)—and the Crafts are readily mentioned. By contrast, in the scholarship on the slave narrative as an American literary genre, omission of their book has been common.

The significance of this University of Georgia Press Brown Thrasher edition is that it reclaims the Crafts' narrative as both literature and literary history. As literature, *Running* pushes us to look more distantly, beyond America, for clues to the origins and influences of the slave narratives. Also, it invites us to observe more closely the form and language decisions made by African American authors, so we may know what these narratives have to say about the dreams of those who invented them. As literary history, *Running* and the events that constitute its prelude and its aftermath demonstrate the complex, contradictory ways in which fugitives like the Crafts composed, manufactured, packaged, sold, and even resold themselves to middle-class nineteenth-century black and white audiences. Both the two-part narrative and its two stars, finally, orient us to the complexities and contradictions which may surface as we reconcile the stories of such fugitive slaves to popular visual, lyrical, and literary images of blackness.

Poster children for both African insurgence and American respectability, the Georgia-born Crafts rose from the obscurity of bondage to the notoriety of fame in an escape that began twelve years prior to *Running*'s initial publication. They left the South in 1848, when to them it was "the gloomy prison / Darken'd by the nation's crime,"[2] and where its mostly rural economy was supported by the toils, as William says,[3] of over two million "over-worked, under-fed, and frequently unmercifully flogged" slaves. A few years before the Crafts' 1848 flight, Frederick Douglass had escaped Maryland and had purchased his own freedom with £150 (approximately six hundred dollars) raised by British supporters. With Martin R. Delany, the tinderbox black nationalist, he had started publishing the *North Star* (1845), a weekly antislavery newspaper, in Rochester, New York. William Wells Brown, another important fugitive who would later become the Crafts' dear confidante and friend, had published the second edition of his best-selling *Narrative* (1847). Rebellions had been led by American slaves such as Nat Turner of Virginia (1831) and Denmark Vesey of South Carolina (1822) and by kidnapped Africans aboard the slave ships *Amistad* (1839) and *Creole* (1841). Along with the growth of maroon or runaway communities in areas like the Great Dismal Swamp, all these undermined popular sentiments that bondage consisted of the "pleasant homes" of kind mistresses, soft masters, and happy, contented black chattel. Like parting curtains in a window, black and white abolitionist authors such as Frances Ellen Watkins Harper and Lydia Maria Child had further affirmed that the shimmering South really was a sham.[4]

The Crafts met in central Georgia's fertile cotton country. The striking, near-white Ellen—who was owned by her father, the planter James P. Smith—had lived in the town of Clinton since birth. Her mother, a mulatto named Maria, was also Smith's slave. Finely prized for her sewing, Ellen had been given at eleven years of age to one of her white half-sisters, Eliza, who had married Robert Collins, a wealthy Macon landholder, city father, and entrepreneur.[5] The anguish of Ellen's separation from her mother must have been excruciating. It was relieved only by the knowledge that she would no longer have to endure what William calls the "incessant cruelty" of her former mistress, who had been embarrassed by the family resemblance etched for all to see in Ellen's features. Ellen's story, then, repeated the same, shocking, "tangled genealogies" that by 1860 were stock-in-trade of professional fugitives' tales.

A carpenter, William was the property of another Macon citizen. Like Ellen's, his childhood had been scarred by terror, separation, violence, and insult. One by one, he tells us, his family had been "knocked down," or auctioned off, in order to settle his old master's debts or just because they were getting old and the vulgar master did not want the burden of caring for them. It therefore came as no surprise when William himself became bank property after his master lost badly in cotton speculations. Like many slave artisans—blacksmiths, cobblers, bricklayers, wheelwrights—William's skills were in wide demand by less-prosperous farmers and townspeople who lacked capable labor in these areas; so he was very probably "hired out," and moved rather unmolested in the region. Probably to emphasize how slaves like him and Ellen were little more than machines to their owners, William omits details about the couple's initial encounters and romance. Instead, he includes examples of the "legal as well as social tyranny" that drives him and Ellen to flee. The combination of his mobility, Ellen's nimble fingers, their privileged positions as house slaves, and the money they had managed to salt away supported them in a brash, impassioned escape.

Ellen stitched trousers and cut her hair. She donned overcoat, hat, cravat, boots, and other particulars of a man's wardrobe, which William had purchased intermittently at various locations to avoid incurring suspicion of escape. With the finishing touches of a sling for her "rheumatic" right hand (to avoid having to sign her name at hotel registers, since she could not write), a cane in the other to support a frail shuffle, and dramatic green spectacles and bandages to distract from the smooth, feminine contours of her face, Ellen transformed into the aristocratic, eccentric, yet invalid young white planter named Mr. Johnson. The only finery that William, on the other hand, troubled himself with was the purchase of a saucy beaver hat. Since his darker skin would cause southerners to assume that he must be someone's property, he astutely elected to accompany Ellen dressed in more motley attire, to perfect the masquerade as his "master's" loyal slave valet.

They would say, should the curious inquire of them, that the purpose of their journey from Atlanta was to find relief for Ellen's ailments by consulting a specialist in Philadelphia. For the most part, Ellen planned to deter conversation and evade scrutiny by feigning deafness, toothache, and snobbery. "[S]mart, active, and exceedingly attentive to his young master—indeed, he was almost eyes, ears, hands and feet for him,"[6] William would serve Ellen so ardently that his obeisance and loyalty, even more so than the cast of his skin, would safeguard his disguise.

For days, as their narrative states, the pair traveled north, primarily by boat and rail. Their route traced east by stage to the "Wall Street of the South," Savannah, thus dubbed because of its lively cotton exchange. Then they journeyed north by the steamer *General Clinch* to Charleston, by another steamer to Wilmington, by trains through Richmond, Baltimore, and Havre de Grace, on ferry across the Susquehanna, and then by train to Philadelphia. Ellen the master relaxed whenever she could in private hotel apartments. Prohibited by slave codes from sitting and sleeping within the same first-class accommodations reserved for whites like his "massa," William the slave bunked wherever he could, usually on stacks of stowed baggage. In spite of temporary separations—and frightening close calls with travelers who suspected their true identities— the Crafts arrived in Philadelphia, as William writes, on Christmas Sunday 1848. Ellen was about twenty-two years old, William, twenty-four.[7]

By early January 1849, the Crafts were residing in Boston's small but close-knit African American community, where William quickly installed himself in a rather prosperous furniture business of his own. Guided by such antislavery grandees as the professional fugitive William Wells Brown, the Underground Railroad conductor Lewis Hayden, and the Unitarian minister Samuel J. May, the glamorous and romantic pair were doted upon by abolitionists. They were frequently presented to audiences at packed meetings of the Massachusetts Anti-Slavery Society in historic Tremont Temple and Faneuil Hall. As the couple electrified venues throughout the strongly abolitionist state, the press tracked their movements in its periodicals: the *Non-Slaveholder* and *Pennsylvania Freeman* (Philadelphia), the *National Anti-Slavery Standard* (New York), the *Daily Mercury* (Newark), the *Free-Soiler, Daily Journal,* and *Commonwealth* (Boston), and, of course, the *Liberator* (founded in Boston in 1831), the most widely circulating and longest-running abolitionist newspaper.

These papers reveled in exposing details that would stick in any southerner's craw. They reported, for example, how the illiterate Crafts had stayed at the very same high-toned Charleston hotel favored by Senator John C. Calhoun, slavery's defender of states' rights (his home state of South Carolina was first to secede from the Union) and a spitfire believer in the divinely ordained inferiority of black people.

Yet the capacious reception of the Crafts up north was met in 1850 by a national counteroffensive designed to yank renegade bodies like theirs right back into servitude. Angered because some of the new western territories acquired during the Mexican War (1846–48) might be declared off-limits to slavery, southern states pressured Congress to ratify a special bill—or else they would secede. In a compromise measure with sectionalists that, in *Running*, William can only describe as "an enactment too infamous to have been thought of or tolerated by any people in the world, except the unprincipled and tyrannical Yankees," Congress passed the Fugitive Slave Act. This prohibited residents of the free states from harboring or extending aid to fugitive slaves, and it gave incentives to judges, federal marshals, and other officials to extend legal assistance and protection to southerners desirous of recovering their lost property. Ultimately, anyone caught trying to thwart its execution could be punished with as much as a six-month jail sentence and a two-thousand-dollar fine. Any blacks arrested as a consequence of the law were not entitled to defend themselves in court.

In the wake of the Fugitive Slave Act, hundreds of fugitives in the northeast and mid-west elected to leave what most had called the "nominally free" northern states for more tranquil settlements in Ontario and Nova Scotia, Canada. Those who remained, such as Frederick Jenkins, Thomas Sims, and Anthony Burns, often were arrested and re-enslaved, even as citizens assaulted federal troops, stormed jails, and jammed their boats up in bays in order to prevent such travesties. Handbills designed by the famous Unitarian minister Theodore Parker circulated throughout Boston, cautioning everyone to "Keep a Sharp Look Out for KIDNAPPERS, and have TOP EYE open." For there were mounting cases of the disappearances of freeborn African Americans—especially women and children—who had been seized by bounty hunters and whisked summarily into slavery, without any opportunity to establish their true identities, or to exchange good-byes freely with relatives and friends.

Inevitably, with the written endorsement of President Fillmore himself, the Crafts' indignant owners commissioned the slavehunters Willis H. Hughes and John Knight, one the Macon jailer and the other a carpenter who knew William, to travel to Boston with an arrest warrant, seize the couple, and return them to bondage. A biracial Committee of Vigilance quickly mobilized to rescue the Crafts and run the "ruffians" out of town. Hughes and Knight were harassed, roughed up, jailed numerous times, and, finally, run out of town. However, knowing that they would never completely evade what Douglass in his *Narrative* called the "painful liability to be returned again to slavery," the Crafts astutely realized that their victory was a temporary one. In November 1850 they fled Boston, and in early December they disembarked from the steamer *Cambria* in Liverpool harbor. Here in England, where in 1838 Parliament had abolished slavery in its Caribbean colonies, their narrative closes, after brief expressions of gratitude to the aristocrats, reformers, beaux mondes, and other British antislavery friends who assisted them in making new lives abroad.

"When I heard of the passage of the fugitive slave bill," wrote William Wells Brown, "I had some faint hope that the people there would protect those who had fled to that city for safety. But when I heard of the flight of the Crafts, I gave up all hopes of the fugitives being safe on any soil over which the 'stars and stripes' float."[8] The Crafts' exodus from America stresses a theme of national disorder that the topsy-turvy structure of their narrative underscores. Where the first section of *Running* begins in the supposedly benevolent institution of southern slavery, it ends with the couple securing real happiness only in the North. One would expect the second part to celebrate the Crafts' newfound freedom. Instead, it tracks the couple's hasty route to Maine, then Nova Scotia, and, finally, England, as they flee from remandment into servitude. It focuses on how tentative liberty is, how the Crafts are "free from every slavish fear" only after leaving America, and how "it is well known in England, if not all over the world, that the Americans, as a people, are notoriously mean and cruel towards all colored persons, whether they are bond or free."

Once the Crafts arrived in England, why did a decade pass before their narrative appeared? As William states, he and Ellen first had "to acquire a little of that education which we were so shamefully deprived of while in the house of bondage." They succeeded quite well at the experimental Ockham School outside London, which they attended for three years under the patronage of Lady Byron and where they were briefly employed. Ellen bore five children: Charles Estlin Phillips, William, Brougham, Alfred, and Ellen. William worked on *Running* and tried his hand at operating various businesses. From their West London residence, both devoted their energies to the work of the London Emancipation Committee and other overseas outposts of Garrisonian abolition.

However, what proved most prosperous to the Crafts in their expatriate years was their following in the footsteps of William Wells Brown, the flamboyant Henry "Box" Brown, Douglass, and the other old hands who had molded themselves into professional refugees on the British and American antislavery lecture or lyceum circuit. From February to May 1849, William Wells Brown had lectured with the couple on a four-month tour of Massachusetts and Connecticut. In his biography of William Wells Brown, William Edward Farrison writes, "Brown and the Crafts followed a simple routine for their meetings. First, with appropriate remarks—which were seldom brief—Brown introduced Craft, who recounted his and his wife's lives as slaves and their escape from slavery. As Craft became more accustomed to facing audiences, he lengthened his story until he usually took about an hour to tell it. Next Brown delivered a speech whose purpose was critical and persuasive, and which lasted about an hour. After this he introduced Mrs. Craft, who sometimes added a few words to what her husband had said. Occasionally Brown sang a song or two. Finally a collection for the antislavery cause was taken, abolition publications were offered for sale, and the meeting was adjourned."[9] If England were now "that country to which young American gentlemen go to increase their stock of knowledge, to seek pleasure, to have their rough, democratic manners softened by contact with English aristocratic refinement,"[10] then the Crafts intended to embarrass the United States of America for assuming Britain's former role of tyrant. They were the first casualties of the Fugitive Slave Act to seek protection under the Union Jack, and the first husband-and-wife team of American slaves to manage a British tour. Their typical path included such northern English factory cities as Liverpool, Manchester, Birmingham, and Leeds; resorts and ports like Bath and Bristol; Glasgow, Edinburgh, and Aberdeen, Scotland; and, framing the whole progress, the bustling capital of London in the country's southern tip.

By 1860, all this had brought them to the attention of the London publisher William Tweedie, who distributed the monthly *Anti-Slavery Advocate* for the Anglo-American Anti-Slavery Association. In tandem with sketches of Ellen in her masculine attire that circulated throughout the 1850s, *Running* would use ironic scenes of reversal and disguise to expose the nineteenth century's attitudes towards sexuality and race. Both of these demonstrate how shifting national dialogues on femininity, masculinity, blackness, and whiteness shaped the reception of fugitives like the Crafts. They also show us how the fugitives represented themselves, even as abolitionism appropriated, regulated, or even stereotyped them.

If, as antebellum fugitive narratives go, *Running* came late to the table, it certainly chose an auspicious year to arrive. The slave population had doubled to over four million: every seventh American was enslaved. "Agitate! Agitate! Agitate!" Douglass had commanded his fellow reformers.[11] "What saved William and Ellen

Craft?" they had responded, "AGITATION. [W]hat practically and peacably [*sic*] nullified the [fugitive slave] law? AGITATION."[12] And they looked poised to win. By 1860, John Brown's body lay "a mouldering in the grave," Civil War loomed, and abolitionists on both continents leveled slavery's deathblows in an even more intensive outpouring of both literature and illustration.

As William Still's compendious *Underground Rail Road* (1872) shows, men escaped slavery disguised as women, women escaped slavery concealed under masculine clothes, mothers escaped with children, and husbands ran away with wives more frequently than their enemies would have anticipated. Yet the Crafts' escape remained enchanting to nineteenth-century British and American readers. With *The Stars and Stripes* (1858), her drama based on the couple's run for freedom, Lydia Maria Child must have attracted more public interest in a written version told by the Crafts themselves. The nineteenth chapter of William Wells Brown's wildly popular *Clotel* (1853) compounded publicity about the Crafts on both sides of the Atlantic and kept their story alive. In a scene Brown must have heard at least a thousand times as he sat with the Crafts at meetings, a "tall," dark-skinned slave named William, "whose countenance beamed with intelligence," colludes with the fair-complexioned Clotel (whom readers would recognize as Ellen) to escape—she disguised as a planter, and he as her slave. She is gentlemanly in "a neat suit of black" and green eyeglasses; "playing his part well in the servant's hall," he escorts her (172).

Even the original Jewett edition of Harriet Stowe's blockbuster *Uncle Tom's Cabin* (1852), which in its heyday "sold more copies than any book in the world except the Bible,"[13] reminded audiences of the Crafts' tenacious escape—and probably left them wondering where the firsthand version was. In the chapter entitled "Liberty," the slave mother Eliza, whose flight with her infant Harry across the ice floes of the Ohio inspired poems, songs, and paintings, flees to Canada disguised as a white man. Accompanying her, of course, is her beloved son "dressed in girl's clothes."

This flurry of interest by other authors certainly must have compensated for any money, converts, or wonder lost by sidelining *Running*'s publication. Engravings of Ellen which depicted her as a "Female Slave in Male Attire, Fleeing as a Planter," also kept her in front of the voyeuristic eyes of abolition, even as she juggled her public roles as speaker and activist with the private obligations of mother and wife. In 1857, for example, the Leeds Anti-Slavery Association sold an illustrated, youth edition of *Uncle Tom's Cabin* on the same page as a notice for a shilling portrait of Ellen wearing masculine garments. Like the signed, engraved portrait of the narrator that typically graces the first-person story of a fugitive slave, the drawing of Ellen reminded observers that her bizarre and harrowing journey had really taken place.

It also exploited a national obsession. The nineteenth century was a time when spectacle was everything, and a time when droves of spectacles—minstrel shows, world's fairs, Wild West productions, jubilees, Dime Museums, fugitive slave exhibits—not only entertained and shocked viewers, but also projected their fears, prejudices, hostilities, and other anxieties. From confidence men to mountain men, from decorated soldiers to ne'er-do-wells, white American women who "unsexed" themselves and "reversed" their genders by putting on pants and other masculine apparel—such as Amelia Bloomer, the leader of the dress reform movement, and Dr. Mary Edwards Walker, a Civil War surgeon—certainly fitted this category. Their stories often collided with the popular belief that looking like a man meant wanting to be a man—and being and behaving less like a woman. "The apparent fear in nineteenth-century society," writes the historian Gayle V. Fischer, "was that all feminine gender characteristics would disappear when a woman or girl wore the clothes of the opposite sex. Or, even worse, females would 'become' men, for 'clothes are gender.'"[14]

Both black and white women matriculated from colleges, ran businesses, and broke old sanctions against speaking in public and choosing to remain unmarried. Yet nineteenth-century culture cleaved to outworn notions that sexuality, like race, could be rigidly defined and bifurcated by such physical markers as a flowing mane of hair. Any violation of these strict compartments was improper, unnatural, immoral, and destructive. When the Union's victory was imminent, for example, northern papers lampooned southern men and attacked loyal southern women by depicting cartoons of Jefferson Davis, the President of the Confederacy, dressed in petticoats, and using his disguise to beat a permanent retreat from troops of the Grand Old Army.[15] In this context, straight-laced Victorian audiences who identified black women as laboring machines, as prostitutes, or as objects of derision and scorn, may have found it difficult to look at Ellen and discern a lady under the man's top hat, high collar, and tie.

Women who put on men's clothing did not always meet with scandal and disdain. A plucky, independent heroine like Capitola Black of Mrs. E. D. E. N. Southworth's best-seller *The Hidden Hand* (1859), published one year shy of *Running,* is a literary example of this type. Poor, homeless, and alone in the city, she puts on men's clothing for practicality's sake: to make more money as a newsboy (an employment that society denies to proper young women) and to avoid being raped. After her luck turns, however, and she is "transfigured" into a "well and properly attired" young woman, she sits in a stereotyped, yet very appropriate, embarrassment, "deeply blushing at the recollection of her male attire."

Real women cross-dressed, Marjorie Garber explains, not only to gain economic parity with men or to protect themselves from sexual assault.[16] If hunger were enough of an excuse to sanction a woman—actual or invented—to dress in a man's costume, then the equally sterling motives for Ellen's escape must have normalized her cross-dressing (i.e., emphasized it as transitional and motivated by necessity or heterosexual romance) and restored her into womanhood. Her reasons for her flight, after all, link her to the pious, pure, domestic, and submissive "true woman" or "angel of the house" that periodicals like *Godey's Ladies' Book* held up as the standard for antebellum femininity. Middle-class true womanhood depended upon rigid assumptions of unsullied whiteness and corrupting blackness. Antislavery narratives like *Running* thus disturbed this binary by putting forth mulatto slaves who were more modest, motherly, and sacrificing than the truest of true women, even as they ignored real differences between Anglo-Saxon women and their African American sisters.

Because she escaped so that her children would be free, in true womanly fashion Ellen placed others before her own prospects. Because she longed for a real church marriage (she and William, being slaves, had not been permitted one), she confirmed the true woman's role as spiritual center of the household. In its part, to underscore this rationale, *Running* would emphasize how reluctantly Ellen disguised herself as a man, even though it meant that she could finally be free, and how quickly "she threw off the disguise" once they reached safety in Philadelphia. Vindicating her womanhood, Ellen had merely passed as a man, rather than denying her feminineness on a permanent basis.[17]

Throughout the 1850s, the mesmerizing figure of Ellen in her masculine apparel played on racial as well as gendered connotations of passing. Once she spoke, said the *Liberator* (2 March 1849), the question arose, "Is it possible that that creature was ever a slave?" Men's clothing aside, Ellen fit cultural expectations of whiteness because she was intelligent, moral, and civilized: the *Cincinnati Commercial* (14 January 1867) described her as "quite good-looking, quite intelligent, and . . . welcomed in the best society of London." Even more, she could pass as a white woman, albeit she had black blood, and had lived in southern bondage since her birth. In *Running* she escapes as a white man, only to be mistaken for a white woman after she removes her male wardrobe. So, for better or worse, Ellen as a surrogate white woman—and William as a blackened-up white man—became bound in the "logic of mulatto exceptionalism," or what the critic Paul Gilmore has defined as "the idea that blacks displayed admirable traits because of their 'Anglo-Saxon blood.'"[18]

Sometimes *Running* attacks the belief that Ellen's positive qualities derive from her white blood; on other occasions, it invests in it. This recognizes how deeply notions of white supremacy persisted in the national consciousness, even among reformers, and even among abolitionists who worked alongside former slaves. For example, in a celebrated mid-1840s New Orleans court case, a German woman named Salomé Muller successfully testified that she was not a slave by birth, but had been wrongfully set to work as one for twenty-five long years.

What seemed most compelling to nineteenth-century audiences, who were mesmerized by such stories of "white slavery," was what the stories said about the fluidity of race. They were disturbed by how easily a "perfectly white" person like Muller, whose skin was supposed to entitle her to privilege and protection, had been reduced to the stigmatic condition of a slave. Among such American authors as George Washington Cable, Frederick Law Olmsted, and Thomas Bushnell Hart, William Wells Brown would return to her story in "A Free Woman Reduced to Slavery," the fourteenth chapter of his *Clotel*. Also referencing Muller's story, William Craft shows in *Running* that if a white slave trader could be "so totally devoid of all natural affection as to sell his own offspring into returnless bondage," then whiteness and blackness could not be so rigidly distinguished, "as there are good-for-nothing white as well as colored persons everywhere." At the same time, by amplifying the horror of whites remanded as slaves, he relies upon the very same distinctions he intends to criticize.

"In the early 1850s," Gilmore writes, "to depict a black man as a man required either painting him white—as with mulatto heroes—or stripping off his blackness to reveal a white interior. . . . But both solutions replicated the racial distinctions they attempted to question—whiteness made one a man, blackness, by itself, left one less a man" (764). William uses masking and inversion to show how these solutions complicated black masculinity. While he and Ellen are resting in Charleston during their escape, he goes outside to polish Ellen's shoes, where he meets another slave bootblack named Pompey (the name, at least, borrowed from his dear friend's *Clotel*). Linking both the real and the artificial slave to the white man's traits of self-reliance, the "shrewd" Pompey urges his comrade William to escape. However, where William is quiet and reserved, like a "natural" white gentleman, Pompey is loud, effusive, and sentimental, like nineteenth-century notions of the typical degraded black male slave. And Pompey's African vernacular ("By squash!") and mispronunciations ("Philumadelphy" for Philadelphia, for example) remind the literate William "that on the sea coast of South Carolina and Georgia the slaves speak worse English than in any other part of the country." Pompey's talk about escape seems more counterfeit than committed (he wears "an air of independence," and he cries when William leaves), whereas we know that the intrepid William has already done the deed, and passes only momentarily as a slave.

This exchange thus distances William from the worst effects of slavery (i.e., making one unmanly), and it situates his behavior within acceptable social codes that connect white masculinity with literacy, courage, self-reliance, and power. At the same time, William shows, slavery has disadvantaged them both. "[J]ust as I took the boots up and started off," he writes, Pompey "caught my hand between his two, and gave it a hearty shake, and, with tears streaming down his cheeks, said: 'God bless you, broder.'" They share an understanding that being a black man means resisting victimization, even though William's travels, education, and professional fugitive status pressure him to conform like Ellen to white codes of sexuality that erase other parts of himself. William responds, "I was afraid to say much to him, but I shall never forget his earnest request, nor fail to do what little I can to release the millions of unhappy bondmen, of whom he was one." His statement once again admits that he, after all, challenges the common portrayal of the enslaved black men for whom he speaks: that they are all illiterate, cowardly, dependent, and weak. He also alludes to the ironies of a privileged, literate former slave like himself speaking for those voiceless masses still in southern bondage, a theme that anticipates the post-Reconstruction writings of W. E. B. Du Bois, Anna Julia Cooper, and Frances E. W. Harper.

Where William might have hesitated to speak on behalf of so many, the British press was not as reluctant to offer its opinions of his narrative. The *Anti-Slavery Advocate* (2 July 1860) praised it as "very entertaining"; and the *Anti-Slavery Reporter* (June 1860) expressed confidence that the narrative "will do some good, by exposing the utter misery which slaves endure, even when not under bad masters, nor badly treated." After *Running*'s publication, the story of the Crafts' escape would be rewritten and even fictionalized by such luminaries as Josephine Brown, William Wells Brown's daughter; Colonel Thomas Wentworth Higginson, Emily Dickinson's confidante; and the Harlem Renaissance writer Georgia Douglas Johnson.

Remarkably, the Crafts' story ends where it began — in Georgia. After a nineteen-year tenure in exile, they returned to a Georgia that was very much the same as it was when slavery had started. It was not as if their times abroad had been dull. Ellen had been reunited with her mother, who had purchased her own freedom; then she had become the center of a scandal in which the southern papers said that she missed her old master and wanted to return to him. William had traveled extensively in western Africa, trying to encourage the residents to grow their own cotton and break the back of the American plantation economy. At the bustling London World's Fair of 1851, both Ellen and William had strolled the exhibits arm-in-arm with white abolitionists. They had used their own slaves' bodies to protest the bondage of black men and women, which undermined the Fair's themes of enlightenment and progress. But by the 1870s, the South again beckoned to exiles like the Crafts who would put their talents to use by assisting the newly emancipated slaves. This strategy, called race uplift, meant transforming the slaves into citizens with a four-part agenda focusing on education, land ownership, family, and religion. So, the Crafts returned. They purchased eighteen hundred acres of land near Savannah to establish a vocational school for the state's freedmen and freedwomen.

Running reminds us of the important fact that abolition was a transatlantic affair, a dynamic and boisterous movement in which many different coalitions of nations, races, and genders were involved. Because it directs our attention to how fugitive slaves made their way through shifting attitudes toward gender and race, the saga of the Crafts' incredible escape retains the qualities that once had compelled nineteenth-century audiences to read it. *Running* also demonstrates how the narratives of fugitive slaves shaped other British and American writings, and were themselves the products of many streams of literature. We may treasure it, however, for reasons that may be less scholarly than the aforesaid, but by no means less important. This is not a depressing tale of violence and victimization; instead, it focuses on the Crafts' spectacular adventure. It is a love story. It is a daring and suspenseful one, where truth is stranger than fiction. And, it is an inspiration. As one of the most spirited and charming accounts from nineteenth-century literature and history, *Running* deserves its place on our bookshelves and in our classrooms.

NOTES

1. See Arna Bontemps, *Great Slave Narratives* (Boston: Beacon Press, 1969), 1; and Henry Louis Gates Jr., introduction to *The Classic Slave Narratives* (New York: New American Library, 1987), xi.

2. From Frances Ellen Watkins Harper's poem "President Lincoln's Proclamation of Freedom," in *A Brighter Coming Day: A Frances Ellen Watkins Harper Reader,* ed. Frances Smith Foster (New York: Feminist Press, 1990), 186–87.

3. *Running*'s first person narrator is William, and he also signs his name as author of its preface, which is consistent in tone and style with the

rest of the book. This indicates that he may have been *Running*'s primary narrator, or that he very likely wrote the whole book himself. All the reviews of *Running* in the transatlantic abolitionist press that I have found attribute sole authorship of *Running* to William.

4. Harper's newly rediscovered novel *Minnie's Sacrifice* (1867) uses the familiar convention of "slavery's pleasant homes" to show that the South merely pretended to treat its slave populations kindly. In such stories as "Slavery's Pleasant Homes" (1843) and "Annette Gray" (1841), Child's use of similar meanings adds poignancy to the tragic lives of beautiful mulatto heroines. See *Three Rediscovered Novels by Frances E. W. Harper*, ed. Frances Smith Foster (Boston: Beacon Press, 1994), 1–92; and *A Lydia Maria Child Reader*, ed. Carolyn Karcher (Durham, N.C.: Duke University Press, 1997), 238–42, 200–208.

5. The most exhaustive historical essay on William Craft (1824–1900) and Ellen Craft (1826–90) is Richard J. M. Blackett's "The Odyssey of William and Ellen Craft," in his *Beating against the Barriers: Biographical Essays on Nineteenth-Century Afro-American History* (Baton Rouge: Louisiana State University Press, 1986), 87–137. Biographical details on the Crafts are also compiled from Florence B. Freedman, introduction to *Running a Thousand Miles for Freedom* (reprint, New York: Arno Press and the *New York Times*, 1969), i–xix, and Dorothy Sterling, "Ellen Craft: The Valiant Journey," in her *Black Foremothers: Three Lives*, 2d ed. (Old Westbury, N.Y.: Feminist Press, 1988), 3–59; the five volumes of C. Peter Ripley et al., eds., *The Black Abolitionist Papers* (Chapel Hill: University of North Carolina Press, 1985; hereafter cited as *BAP*); and Benjamin Quarles, *Black Abolitionists* (New York: Oxford University Press, 1969).

6. William Still, *The Underground Rail Road* (Philadelphia, 1872), 369.

7. While four days is how long the narrative says their journey lasted, contemporaneous accounts by the northern abolitionist community contradict this claim. The Crafts planned the escape for four days and reached Philadelphia in four more, "eight days after it was first thought of." The time of their arrival in the City of Brotherly Love perhaps may stand as a romantic example of the kind of artistic license typically employed in fugitive slaves' narratives, where success in convincing readers of the injustice of southern bondage often necessitated bending the truth a little — especially if innocent lives hung in the balance, or if adherence to the requirements of strict authenticity risked downplaying the horrors of the ordeal.

8. Letter of William Wells Brown to the *North Star*, 16 January 1851, document 31 in *The British Isles, 1830 -1865*, vol. 1 of *BAP*.

9. William Edward Farrison, *William Wells Brown, Author and Reformer* (Chicago: University of Chicago Press, 1969), 136-37.

10. Frederick Douglass, *My Bondage and My Freedom* (New York: Literary Classics of the United States, 1994), 370.

11. Frederick Voss, *Majestic in His Wrath: A Pictorial History of the Life of Frederick Douglass* (Washington, D.C.: Smithsonian Institution, 1995), 83.

12. "Final Flight of the Slave Hunter.—A Precious Confession." *Free-Soiler*, 2 Nov. 1850: 3.

13. Elizabeth Ammons, introduction to *Uncle Tom's Cabin; Or, Life among the Lowly* (New York: Norton, 1994), viii.

14. Gayle V. Fischer, "A Matter of Wardrobe?: Mary Edwards Walker, a Nineteenth-Century American Cross-Dresser," *Fashion Theory* (forthcoming).

15. See Nina Silber, *The Romance of Reunion: Northerners and the South, 1865 -1900* (Chapel Hill: University of North Carolina Press, 1993), 13-38.

16. See Marjorie Garber, *Vested Interests: Cross-Dressing and Cultural Anxiety* (New York: Routledge, 1992).

17. For more on Ellen Craft and the cult of true womanhood, see my essays "Ellen Craft—The Fugitive as Text and Artifact," *African American Review* 28:4 (winter 1994): 509-29; and " 'Trust No Man!' But What about a Woman?: Ellen Craft and a Genealogical Model for Teaching Douglass' *Narrative*," in *Approaches to Teaching the Narrative of the Life of Frederick Douglass,* ed. James C. Hall (New York: MLA, forthcoming).

18. Paul Gilmore, " 'De Genewine Artekil': William Wells Brown, Blackface Minstrelsy, and Abolitionism," *American Literature* 69:4 (December 1997): 743-80.

"Slaves cannot breathe in England: if their lungs
Receive our air, that moment they are free;
They touch our country, and their shackles fall."

COWPER

RUNNING

A THOUSAND

MILES FOR

FREEDOM

PREFACE

Having heard while in Slavery that "God made of one blood all nations of men," and also that the American Declaration of Independence says, that "We hold these truths to be self-evident, that all men are created equal; that they are endowed by their Creator with certain inalienable rights; that among these, are life, liberty, and the pursuit of happiness;" we could not understand by what right we were held as "chattels." Therefore, we felt perfectly justified in undertaking the dangerous and exciting task of "running a thousand miles" in order to obtain those rights which are so vividly set forth in the Declaration. I beg those who would know the particulars of our journey, to peruse these pages. This book is not intended as a full history of the life of my wife, nor of myself; but merely as an account of our escape; together with other matter which I hope may be the means of creating in some minds a deeper abhorrence of the sinful and abominable practice of enslaving and brutifying our fellow-creatures. Without stopping to write a long apology for offering this little volume to the public, I shall commence at once to pursue my simple story.

W. CRAFT

12, Cambridge Road,
Hammersmith,
London

Part I

"God gave us only over beast, fish, fowl,
Dominion absolute; that right we hold
By his donation. But man over man
He made not lord; such title to himself
Reserving, human left from human free."

MILTON

M y wife and myself were born in different towns in the State of Georgia, which is one of the principal slave States. It is true, our condition as slaves was not by any means the worst; but the mere idea that we were held as chattels, and deprived of all legal rights—the thought that we had to give up our hard earnings to a tyrant, to enable him to live in idleness and luxury—the thought that we could not call the bones and sinews that God gave us our own: but above all, the fact that another man had the power to tear from our cradle the new-born babe and sell it in the shambles like a brute, and then scourge us if we dared to lift a finger to save it from such a fate, haunted us for years.

But in December, 1848, a plan suggested itself that proved quite successful, and in eight days after it was first thought of we were free from the horrible trammels of slavery, rejoicing and praising God in the glorious sunshine of liberty.

My wife's first master was her father, and her mother his slave, and the latter is still the slave of his widow.

Notwithstanding my wife being of African extraction on her mother's side, she is almost white—in fact, she is so nearly so that the tyrannical old lady to whom she first belonged became so annoyed, at finding her frequently mistaken for a child of the family, that she gave her when eleven years of age to a daughter, as a wedding present. This separated my wife from her mother, and also from several other dear friends. But the incessant cruelty of her old mistress made the change of owners or treatment so desirable, that she did not grumble much at this cruel separation.

It may be remembered that slavery in America is not at all confined to persons of any particular complexion; there are a very large number of slaves as white as any one; but as the evidence of a slave is not admitted in court against a free white person, it is almost impossible for a white child, after having been kidnapped and sold into or reduced to slavery, in a part of the country where it is not known (as often is the case), ever to recover its freedom.

I have myself conversed with several slaves who told me that their parents were white and free; but that they were stolen away from them and sold when quite young. As they could not tell their address, and also as the parents did not know what had become of their lost and dear little ones, of course all traces of each other were gone.

The following facts are sufficient to prove, that he who has the power, and is inhuman enough to trample upon the sacred rights of the weak, cares nothing for race or colour:—

In March, 1818, three ships arrived at New Orleans, bringing several hundred German emigrants from the province of Alsace, on the lower Rhine. Among them were Daniel Muller and his two daughters, Dorothea and Salomé, whose mother had died on the passage. Soon after his arrival, Muller, taking with him his two daughters, both young children, went up the river to Attakapas parish, to work on the plantation of John F. Miller. A few weeks later, his relatives, who had remained at New Orleans, learned that he had died of the fever of the country. They immediately sent for the two girls; but they had disappeared, and the relatives, notwithstanding repeated and persevering inquiries and researches, could find no traces of them. They were at length given up for dead. Dorothea was never again heard of; nor was any thing known of Salomé from 1818 till 1843.

In the summer of that year, Madame Karl, a German woman

who had come over in the same ship with the Mullers, was passing through a street in New Orleans, and accidentally saw Salomé in a wine-shop, belonging to Louis Belmonte, by whom she was held as a slave. Madame Karl recognised her at once, and carried her to the house of another German woman, Mrs. Schubert, who was Salomé's cousin and godmother, and who no sooner set eyes on her than, without having any intimation that the discovery had been previously made, she unhesitatingly exclaimed, "My God! here is the long-lost Salomé Muller."

The *Law Reporter,* in its account of this case, says:—

"As many of the German emigrants of 1818 as could be gathered together were brought to the house of Mrs. Schubert, and every one of the number who had any recollection of the little girl upon the passage, or any acquaintance with her father and mother, immediately identified the woman before them as the long-lost Salomé Muller. By all these witnesses, who appeared at the trial, the identity was fully established. The family resemblance in every feature was declared to be so remarkable, that some of the witnesses did not hesitate to say that they should know her among ten thousand; that they were as certain the plaintiff was Salomé Muller, the daughter of Daniel and Dorothea Muller, as of their own existence."

Among the witnesses who appeared in Court was the midwife who had assisted at the birth of Salomé. She testified to the existence of certain peculiar marks upon the body of the child, which were found, exactly as described, by the surgeons who were appointed by the Court to make an examination for the purpose.

There was no trace of African descent in any feature of Salomé Muller. She had long, straight, black hair, hazel eyes, thin lips, and a Roman nose. The complexion of her face and neck was as dark as that of the darkest brunette. It appears, however, that, during the twenty-five years of her servitude, she had been exposed to the sun's rays in the hot climate of Louisiana, with head and neck unsheltered, as is customary with the female slaves, while labouring in the cotton or the sugar field. Those parts of her person which had been shielded from the sun were comparatively white.

Belmonte, the pretended owner of the girl, had obtained possession of her by an act of sale from John F. Miller, the planter in whose service Salomé's father died. This Miller was a man of consideration and substance, owning large sugar estates, and bearing a high reputation for honour and honesty, and for indulgent treatment of his slaves. It was testified on the trial that he had said to Belmonte, a few weeks after the sale of Salomé, "that she was white, and had as much right to her freedom as any one, and was only to be retained in slavery by care and kind treatment." The broker who negotiated the sale from Miller to Belmonte, in 1838, testified in Court that he then thought, and still thought, that the girl was white!

The case was elaborately argued on both sides, but was at length decided in favour of the girl, by the Supreme Court declaring that "she was free and white, and therefore unlawfully held in bondage."

The Rev. George Bourne, of Virginia, in his *Picture of Slavery*, published in 1834, relates the case of a white boy who, at the age of seven, was stolen from his home in Ohio, tanned and stained in such a way that he could not be distinguished from a person of colour, and then sold as a slave in Virginia. At the age of twenty, he made his escape, by running away, and happily succeeded in rejoining his parents.

I have known worthless white people to sell their own free children into slavery; and, as there are good-for-nothing white as well as coloured persons everywhere, no one, perhaps, will wonder at such inhuman transactions: particularly in the Southern States of America, where I believe there is a greater want of humanity and high principle amongst the whites, than among any other civilized people in the world.

I know that those who are not familiar with the working of "the peculiar institution," can scarcely imagine any one so totally devoid of all natural affection as to sell his own offspring into returnless bondage. But Shakespeare, that great observer of human nature, says:—

> "With caution judge of probabilities.
> Things deemed unlikely, e'en impossible,
> Experience often shews us to be true."

My wife's new mistress was decidedly more humane than the majority of her class. My wife has always given her credit for not exposing her to many of the worst features of slavery. For instance, it is a common practice in the slave States for ladies, when angry with their maids, to send them to the calybuce sugar-house, or to some other place established for the purpose of punishing slaves, and have them severely flogged; and I am sorry it is a fact, that the villains to whom those defenceless creatures are sent, not only flog them as they are ordered, but frequently compel them to submit to the greatest indignity. Oh! if there is any one thing under the wide canopy of heaven, horrible enough to stir a man's soul, and to make his very blood boil, it is the thought of his dear wife, his unprotected sister, or his young and virtuous daughters, struggling to save themselves from falling a prey to such demons!

It always appears strange to me that any one who was not born a slaveholder, and steeped to the very core in the demoralizing atmosphere of the Southern States, can in any way palliate slavery. It is still more surprising to see virtuous ladies looking with patience upon, and remaining indifferent to, the existence of a system that exposes nearly two millions of their own sex in the manner I have mentioned, and that too in a professedly free and Christian country. There is, however, great consolation in knowing that God is just, and will not let the oppressor of the weak, and the spoiler of the virtuous, escape unpunished here and hereafter.

I believe a similar retribution to that which destroyed Sodom is hanging over the slaveholders. My sincere prayer is that they may not provoke God, by persisting in a reckless course of wickedness, to pour out his consuming wrath upon them.

I must now return to our history.

My old master had the reputation of being a very humane and Christian man, but he thought nothing of selling my poor old father, and dear aged mother, at separate times, to different persons, to be dragged off never to behold each other again, till summoned to appear before the great tribunal of heaven. But, oh! what a happy meeting it will be on that great day for those faithful souls. I say a happy meeting, because I never saw persons more devoted to the service of God than they. But how will the case stand with those reckless traffickers in human flesh and blood, who plunged the poisonous dagger of separation into those loving hearts which God had for so many years closely joined together—nay, sealed as it were with his own hands for the eternal courts of heaven? It is not for me to say what will become of those heartless tyrants. I must leave them in the hands of an all-wise and just God, who will, in his own good time, and in his own way, avenge the wrongs of his oppressed people.

My old master also sold a dear brother and a sister, in the same manner as he did my father and mother. The reason he assigned for disposing of my parents, as well as of several other aged slaves, was, that "they were getting old, and would soon become valueless in the market, and therefore he intended to sell off all the old stock, and buy in a young lot." A most disgraceful conclusion for a man to come to, who made such great professions of religion!

This shameful conduct gave me a thorough hatred, not for true Christianity, but for slaveholding piety.

My old master, then, wishing to make the most of the rest of his slaves, apprenticed a brother and myself out to learn trades: he to a black-smith, and myself to a cabinet-maker. If a slave has a good trade, he will let or sell for more than a person without one, and many slaveholders have their slaves taught trades on this account. But before our time expired, my old master wanted money; so he sold my brother, and then mortgaged my sister, a dear girl about fourteen years of age, and myself, then about sixteen, to one of the banks, to get money to speculate in cotton. This we knew nothing of at the moment; but time rolled on, the money became due, my master was unable to meet his payments; so the bank had us placed upon the auction stand and sold to the highest bidder.

My poor sister was sold first: she was knocked down to a planter who resided at some distance in the country. Then I was called upon the stand. While the auctioneer was crying the bids, I saw the man that had purchased my sister getting her into a cart, to take her to his home. I at once asked a slave friend who was standing near the platform, to run and ask the gentleman if he would please to wait till I was sold, in order that I might have an opportunity of bidding her good-bye. He sent me word back that he had some distance to go, and could not wait.

I then turned to the auctioneer, fell upon my knees, and humbly prayed him to let me just step down and bid my last sister farewell. But, instead of granting me this request, he grasped me by the neck, and in a commanding tone of voice, and with a violent oath, exclaimed, "Get up! You can do the wench no good; therefore there is no use in your seeing her."

On rising, I saw the cart in which she sat moving slowly off; and, as she clasped her hands with a grasp that indicated despair, and looked pitifully round towards me, I also saw the large silent tears trickling down her cheeks. She made a farewell bow, and buried her face in her lap. This seemed more than I could bear. It appeared to swell my aching heart to its utmost. But before I could fairly recover, the poor girl was gone;—gone, and I have never had the good fortune to see her from that day to this! Perhaps I should have never heard of her again, had it not been for the untiring efforts of my good old mother, who became free a few years ago by purchase, and, after a great deal of difficulty, found my sister residing with a family in Mississippi. My mother at once wrote to me, informing me of the fact, and requesting me to do something to get her free; and I am happy to say that, partly by lecturing occasionally, and through the sale of an engraving of my wife in the disguise in which she escaped, together with the extreme kindness and generosity of Miss Burdett Coutts, Mr. George Richardson of Plymouth, and a few other friends, I have nearly accomplished this. It would be to me a great and ever-glorious achievement to restore my sister to our dear mother, from whom she was forcibly driven in early life.

I was knocked down to the cashier of the bank to which we were mortgaged, and ordered to return to the cabinet shop where I previously worked.

But the thought of the harsh auctioneer not allowing me to bid my dear sister farewell, sent red-hot indignation darting like lightning through every vein. It quenched my tears, and appeared to set my brain on fire, and made me crave for power to avenge our wrongs! But, alas! we were only slaves, and had no legal rights; consequently we were compelled to smother our wounded feelings, and crouch beneath the iron heel of despotism.

I must now give the account of our escape; but, before doing so, it may be well to quote a few passages from the fundamental laws of slavery; in order to give some idea of the legal as well as the social tyranny from which we fled.

According to the law of Louisiana, "A slave is one who is in the power of a master to whom he belongs. The master may sell him, dispose of his person, his industry, and his labour; he can do nothing, possess nothing, nor acquire anything but what must belong to his master."—*Civil Code, art.* 35.

In South Carolina it is expressed in the following language:— "Slaves shall be deemed, sold, taken, reputed and judged in law to be *chattels personal* in the hands of their owners and possessors, and their executors, administrators, and assigns, *to all intents, constructions, and purposes whatsoever.*"—2 *Brevard's Digest,* 229.

The Constitution of Georgia has the following (Art. 4, sec. 12):— "Any person who shall maliciously dismember or deprive a slave of life, shall suffer such punishment as would be inflicted in case the like offence had been committed on a free white person, and on the like proof, except in case of insurrection of such slave, and unless SUCH DEATH SHOULD HAPPEN BY ACCIDENT IN GIVING SUCH SLAVE MODERATE CORRECTION."—*Prince's Digest,* 559.

I have known slaves to be beaten to death, but as they died under "moderate correction," it was quite lawful; and of course the murderers were not interfered with.

"If any slave, who shall be out of the house or plantation where such slave shall live, or shall be usually employed, or without some white person in company with such slave, shall *refuse to submit* to undergo the examination of *any white* person, (let him be ever so drunk or crazy), it shall be lawful for such white person to pursue, apprehend, and moderately correct such slave; and if such slave shall assault and strike such white person, such slave may be *lawfully killed.*"—2 *Brevard's Digest,* 231.

"Provided always," says the law, "that such striking be not done by the command and in the defence of the person or property of the owner, or other person having the government of such slave; in which case the slave shall be wholly excused."

According to this law, if a slave, by the direction of his overseer, strike a white person who is beating said overseer's pig, "the slave shall be wholly excused." But, should the bondman, of his own accord, fight to defend his wife, or should his terrified daughter instinctively raise her hand and strike the wretch who attempts to violate her chastity, he or she shall, saith the model republican law, suffer death.

From having been myself a slave for nearly twenty-three years, I am quite prepared to say, that the practical working of slavery is worse than the odious laws by which it is governed.

At an early age we were taken by the persons who held us as property to Macon, the largest town in the interior of the State of Georgia, at which place we became acquainted with each other for several years before our marriage; in fact, our marriage was postponed for some time simply because one of the unjust and worse than Pagan laws under which we lived compelled all children of slave mothers to follow their condition. That is to say, the father of the slave may be the President of the Republic; but if the mother should be a slave at the infant's birth, the poor child is ever legally doomed to the same cruel fate.

It is a common practice for gentlemen (if I may call them such), moving in the highest circles of society, to be the fathers of children by their slaves, whom they can and do sell with the greatest impunity; and the more pious, beautiful, and virtuous the girls are, the greater the price they bring, and that too for the most infamous purposes.

Any man with money (let him be ever such a rough brute), can buy a beautiful and virtuous girl, and force her to live with him in a criminal connexion; and as the law says a slave shall have no higher appeal than the mere will of the master, she cannot escape, unless it be by flight or death.

In endeavouring to reconcile a girl to her fate, the master sometimes says that he would marry her if it was not unlawful.* However, he will always consider her to be his wife, and will treat her as such; and she, on the other hand, may regard him as her lawful husband; and if they have any children, they will be free and well educated.

I am in duty bound to add, that while a great majority of such men care nothing for the happiness of the women with whom they live, nor for the children of whom they are the fathers, there are those to be found, even in that heterogeneous mass of licentious monsters, who are true to their pledges. But as the woman and her children are legally the property of the man, who stands in the anomalous relation to them of husband and father, as well as master, they are liable to be seized and sold for his debts, should he become involved.

*It is unlawful in the slave States for any one of purely European descent to intermarry with a person of African extraction; though a white man may live with as many coloured women as he pleases without materially damaging his reputation in Southern society.

There are several cases on record where such persons have been sold and separated for life. I know of some myself, but I have only space to glance at one.

I knew a very humane and wealthy gentleman, that bought a woman, with whom he lived as his wife. They brought up a family of children, among whom were three nearly white, well educated, and beautiful girls.

On the father being suddenly killed it was found that he had not left a will; but, as the family had always heard him say that he had no surviving relatives, they felt that their liberty and property were quite secured to them, and, knowing the insults to which they were exposed, now their protector was no more, they were making preparations to leave for a free State.

But, poor creatures, they were soon sadly undeceived. A villain residing at a distance, hearing of the circumstance, came forward and swore that he was a relative of the deceased; and as this man bore, or assumed, Mr. Slator's name, the case was brought before one of those horrible tribunals, presided over by a second Judge Jeffreys, and calling itself a court of justice, but before whom no coloured person, nor an abolitionist, was ever known to get his full rights.

A verdict was given in favour of the plaintiff, whom the better portion of the community thought had wilfully conspired to cheat the family.

The heartless wretch not only took the ordinary property, but actually had the aged and friendless widow, and all her fatherless children, except Frank, a fine young man about twenty-two years of age, and Mary, a very nice girl, a little younger than her brother, brought to the auction stand and sold to the highest bidder. Mrs. Slator had cash enough, that her husband and master left, to purchase the liberty of herself and children; but on her attempting to do so, the pusillanimous scoundrel, who had robbed them of their freedom, claimed the money as his property; and, poor creature, she had to give it up. According to law, as will be seen hereafter, a slave cannot own anything. The old lady never recovered from her sad affliction.

At the sale she was brought up first, and after being vulgarly criticised, in the presence of all her distressed family, was sold to a cotton planter, who said he wanted the "proud old critter to go to his plantation, to look after the little woolly heads, while their mammies were working in the field."

When the sale was over, then came the separation, and

> "O, deep was the anguish of that slave mother's heart,
> When called from her darlings for ever to part;
> The poor mourning mother of reason bereft,
> Soon ended her sorrows, and sank cold in death."

Antoinette, the flower of the family, a girl who was much beloved by all who knew her, for her Christ-like piety, dignity of manner, as well as her great talents and extreme beauty, was bought by an uneducated and drunken slave-dealer.

I cannot give a more correct description of the scene, when she was called from her brother to the stand, than will be found in the following lines —

> "Why stands she near the auction stand?
>   That girl so young and fair;
> What brings her to this dismal place?
>   Why stands she weeping there?
>
> Why does she raise that bitter cry?
>   Why hangs her head with shame,
> As now the auctioneer's rough voice
>   So rudely calls her name!
>
> But see! she grasps a manly hand,
>   And in a voice so low,
> As scarcely to be heard, she says,
>   'My brother, must I go?'

A moment's pause: then, midst a wail
    Of agonizing woe,
His answer falls upon the ear,—
    'Yes, sister, you must go!

No longer can my arm defend,
    No longer can I save
My sister from the horrid fate
    That waits her as a SLAVE!'

Blush, Christian, blush! for e'en the dark
    Untutored heathen see
Thy inconsistency, and lo!
    They scorn thy God, and thee!"

The low trader said to a kind lady who wished to purchase Antoinette out of his hands, "I reckon I'll not sell the smart critter for ten thousand dollars; I always wanted her for my own use." The lady, wishing to remonstrate with him, commenced by saying, "You should remember, Sir, that there is a just God." Hoskens not understanding Mrs. Huston, interrupted her by saying, "I does, and guess its monstrous kind an' him to send such likely niggers for our convenience." Mrs. Huston finding that a long course of reckless wickedness, drunkenness, and vice, had destroyed in Hoskens every noble impulse, left him.

Antoinette, poor girl, also seeing that there was no help for her, became frantic. I can never forget her cries of despair, when Hoskens gave the order for her to be taken to his house, and locked in an upper room. On Hoskens entering the apartment, in a state of intoxication, a fearful struggle ensued. The brave Antoinette broke loose from him, pitched herself head foremost through the window, and fell upon the pavement below.

Her bruised but unpolluted body was soon picked up—restoratives brought—doctor called in; but, alas! it was too late: her pure and noble spirit had fled away to be at rest in those realms of endless bliss, "where the wicked cease from troubling, and the weary are at rest."

Antoinette like many other noble women who are deprived of liberty, still

> "Holds something sacred, something undefiled;
> Some pledge and keepsake of their higher nature.
> And, like the diamond in the dark, retains
> Some quenchless gleam of the celestial light."

On Hoskens fully realizing the fact that his victim was no more, he exclaimed "By thunder I am a used-up man!" The sudden disappointment, and the loss of two thousand dollars, was more than he could endure: so he drank more than ever, and in a short time died, raving mad with *delirium tremens*.

The villain Slator said to Mrs. Huston, the kind lady who endeavoured to purchase Antoinette from Hoskens, "Nobody needn't talk to me 'bout buying them ar likely niggers, for I'm not going to sell em." "But Mary is rather delicate," said Mrs. Huston, "and, being unaccustomed to hard work, cannot do you much service on a plantation." "I don't want her for the field," replied Slator, "but for another purpose." Mrs. Huston understood what this meant, and instantly exclaimed, "Oh, but she is your cousin!" "The devil she is!" said Slator; and added, "Do you mean to insult me, Madam, by saying that I am related to niggers?" "No," replied Mrs. Huston, "I do not wish to offend you, Sir. But wasn't Mr. Slator, Mary's father, your uncle?" "Yes, I calculate he was," said Slator; "but I want you and everybody to understand that I'm no kin to his niggers." "Oh, very well," said Mrs. Huston; adding, "Now what will you take for the poor girl?" "Nothin'," he replied; "for, as I said before, I'm not goin' to sell, so you needn't trouble yourself no more. If the critter behaves herself, I'll do as well by her as any man."

Slator spoke up boldly, but his manner and sheepish look clearly indicated that

"His heart within him was at strife
　　such accursed gains;
For he knew whose passions gave her life,
　　Whose blood ran in her veins."

"The monster led her from the door,
　　He led her by the hand,
To be his slave and paramour
　　In a strange and distant land!"

Poor Frank and his sister were handcuffed together, and confined in prison. Their dear little twin brother and sister were sold, and taken where they knew not. But it often happens that misfortune causes those whom we counted dearest to shrink away; while it makes friends of those whom we least expected to take any interest in our affairs. Among the latter class Frank found two comparatively new but faithful friends to watch the gloomy paths of the unhappy little twins.

In a day or two after the sale, Slator had two fast horses put to a large light van, and placed in it a good many small but valuable things belonging to the distressed family. He also took with him Frank and Mary, as well as all the money for the spoil; and after treating all his low friends and bystanders, and drinking deeply himself, he started in high glee for his home in South Carolina. But they had not proceeded many miles, before Frank and his sister discovered that Slator was too drunk to drive. But he, like most tipsy men, thought he was all right; and as he had with him some of the ruined family's best brandy and wine, such as he had not been accustomed to, and being a thirsty soul, he drank till the reins fell from his fingers, and in attempting to catch them he tumbled out of the vehicle, and was unable to get up. Frank and Mary there and then contrived a plan by which to escape. As they were still handcuffed by one wrist each, they alighted, took from the drunken assassin's pocket the key, undid the iron bracelets, and placed them upon Slator, who was better fitted to wear such ornaments. As the demon lay unconscious of what was taking place, Frank and Mary took from him the large sum of money that was realized at the sale, as well as that which Slator had so very meanly obtained from their poor mother. They then dragged him into the woods, tied him to a tree, and left the inebriated robber to shift for himself, while they made good their escape to Savannah. The fugitives being white, of course no one suspected that they were slaves.

Slator was not able to call any one to his rescue till late the next day; and as there were no railroads in that part of the country at that time, it was not until late the following day that Slator was able to get a party to join him for the chase. A person informed Slator that he had met a man and woman, in a trap, answering to the description of those whom he had lost, driving furiously towards Savannah. So Slator and several slavehunters on horseback started off in full tilt, with their bloodhounds, in pursuit of Frank and Mary.

On arriving at Savannah, the hunters found that the fugitives had sold the horses and trap, and embarked as free white persons, for New York. Slator's disappointment and rascality so preyed upon his base mind, that he, like Judas, went and hanged himself.

As soon as Frank and Mary were safe, they endeavoured to redeem their good mother. But, alas! she was gone; she had passed on to the realm of spirit life.

In due time Frank learned from his friends in Georgia where his little brother and sister dwelt. So he wrote at once to purchase them, but the persons with whom they lived would not sell them. After failing in several attempts to buy them, Frank cultivated large whiskers and moustachios, cut off his hair, put on a wig and glasses, and went down as a white man, and stopped in the neighbourhood where his sister was; and after seeing her and also his little brother, arrangements were made for them to meet at a particular place on a Sunday, which they did, and got safely off.

I saw Frank myself, when he came for the little twins. Though I was then quite a lad, I well remember being highly delighted by hearing him tell how nicely he and Mary had served Slator.

Frank had so completely disguised or changed his appearance that his little sister did not know him, and would not speak till he showed their mother's likeness; the sight of which melted her to tears,—for she knew the face. Frank might have said to her

> "'O, Emma! O, my sister, speak to me!
> Dost thou not know me, that I am thy brother?
> Come to me, little Emma, thou shalt dwell
> With me henceforth, and know no care or want.'
> Emma was silent for a space, as if
> 'Twere hard to summon up a human voice."

Frank and Mary's mother was my wife's own dear aunt.

After this great diversion from our narrative, which I hope dear reader, you will excuse, I shall return at once to it.

My wife was torn from her mother's embrace in childhood, and taken to a distant part of the country. She had seen so many other children separated from their parents in this cruel manner, that the mere thought of her ever becoming the mother of a child, to linger out a miserable existence under the wretched system of American slavery, appeared to fill her very soul with horror; and as she had taken what I felt to be an important view of her condition, I did not, at first, press the marriage, but agreed to assist her in trying to devise some plan by which we might escape from our unhappy condition, and then be married.

We thought of plan after plan, but they all seemed crowded with insurmountable difficulties. We knew it was unlawful for any public conveyance to take us as passengers, without our master's consent. We were also perfectly aware of the startling fact, that had we left without this consent the professional slave-hunters would have soon had their ferocious bloodhounds baying on our track, and in a short time we should have been dragged back to slavery, not to fill the more favourable situations which we had just left, but to be separated for life, and put to the very meanest and most laborious drudgery; or else have been tortured to death as examples, in order to strike terror into the hearts of others, and thereby prevent them from even attempting to escape from their cruel taskmasters. It is a fact worthy of remark, that nothing seems to give the slaveholders so much pleasure as the catching and torturing of fugitives. They had much rather take the keen and poisonous lash, and with it cut their poor trembling victims to atoms, than allow one of them to escape to a free country, and expose the infamous system from which he fled.

The greatest excitement prevails at a slave-hunt. The slaveholders and their hired ruffians appear to take more pleasure in this inhuman pursuit than English sportsmen do in chasing a fox or a stag. Therefore, knowing what we should have been compelled to suffer, if caught and taken back, we were more than anxious to hit upon a plan that would lead us safely to a land of liberty.

But, after puzzling our brains for years, we were reluctantly driven to the sad conclusion, that it was almost impossible to escape from slavery in Georgia, and travel 1,000 miles across the slave States. We therefore resolved to get the consent of our owners, be married, settle down in slavery, and endeavour to make ourselves as comfortable as possible under that system; but at the same time ever to keep our dim eyes steadily fixed upon the glimmering hope of liberty, and earnestly pray God mercifully to assist us to escape from our unjust thraldom.

We were married, and prayed and toiled on till December, 1848, at which time (as I have stated) a plan suggested itself that proved quite successful, and in eight days after it was first thought of we were free from the horrible trammels of slavery, and glorifying God who had brought us safely out of a land of bondage.

Knowing that slaveholders have the privilege of taking their slaves to any part of the country they think proper, it occurred to me that, as my wife was nearly white, I might get her to disguise herself as an invalid gentleman, and assume to be my master, while I could attend as his slave, and that in this manner we might effect our escape. After I thought of the plan, I suggested it to my wife, but at first she shrank from the idea. She thought it was almost impossible for her to assume that disguise, and travel a distance of 1,000 miles across the slave States. However, on the other hand, she also thought of her condition. She saw that the laws under which we lived did not recognize her to be a woman, but a mere chattel, to be bought and sold, or otherwise dealt with as her owner might see fit. Therefore the more she contemplated her helpless condition, the more anxious she was to escape from it. So she said, "I think it is almost too much for us to undertake; however, I feel that God is on our side, and with his assistance, notwithstanding all the difficulties, we shall be able to succeed. Therefore, if you will purchase the disguise, I will try to carry out the plan."

But after I concluded to purchase the disguise, I was afraid to go to any one to ask him to sell me the articles. It is unlawful in Georgia for a white man to trade with slaves without the master's consent. But, notwithstanding this, many persons will sell a slave any article that he can get the money to buy. Not that they sympathize with the slave, but merely because his testimony is not admitted in court against a free white person.

Therefore, with little difficulty I went to different parts of the town, at odd times, and purchased things piece by piece, (except the trowsers which she found necessary to make,) and took them home to the house where my wife resided. She being a ladies' maid, and a favourite slave in the family, was allowed a little room to herself; and amongst other pieces of furniture which I had made in my overtime, was a chest of drawers; so when I took the articles home, she locked them up carefully in these drawers. No one about the premises knew that she had anything of the kind. So when we fancied we had everything ready the time was fixed for the flight. But we knew it would not do to start off without first getting our master's consent to be away for a few days. Had we left without this, they would soon have had us back into slavery, and probably we should never have got another fair opportunity of even attempting to escape.

Some of the best slaveholders will sometimes give their favourite slaves a few days' holiday at Christmas time; so, after no little amount of perseverance on my wife's part, she obtained a pass from her mistress, allowing her to be away for a few days. The cabinet-maker with whom I worked gave me a similar paper, but said that he needed my services very much, and wished me to return as soon as the time granted was up. I thanked him kindly; but somehow I have not been able to make it convenient to return yet; and, as the free air of good old England agrees so well with my wife and our dear little ones, as well as with myself, it is not at all likely we shall return at present to the "peculiar institution" of chains and stripes.

On reaching my wife's cottage she handed me her pass, and I showed mine, but at that time neither of us were able to read them. It is not only unlawful for slaves to be taught to read, but in some of the States there are heavy penalties attached, such as fines and imprisonment, which will be vigorously enforced upon any one who is humane enough to violate the so-called law.

The following case will serve to show how persons are treated in the most enlightened slaveholding community.

"INDICTMENT.

COMMONWEALTH OF VIRGINIA, NORFOLK COUNTY, ss.}

In the Circuit Court. The Grand Jurors empannelled and sworn to inquire of offences committed in the body of the said County on their oath present, that Margaret Douglass, being an evil disposed person, not having the fear of God before her eyes, but moved and instigated by the devil, wickedly, maliciously, and feloniously, on the fourth day of July, in the year of our Lord one thousand eight hundred and fifty-four, at Norfolk, in said County, did teach a certain black girl named Kate to read in the Bible, to the great displeasure of Almighty God, to the pernicious example of others in like case offending, contrary to the form of the statute in such case made

and provided, and against the peace and dignity of the Commonwealth of
Virginia.

"VICTOR VAGABOND, *Prosecuting Attorney.*"

"On this indictment Mrs. Douglass was arraigned as a necessary matter of
form, tried, found guilty of course; and Judge Scalawag, before whom she
was tried, having consulted with Dr. Adams, ordered the sheriff to place
Mrs. Douglass in the prisoner's box, when he addressed her as follows:
'Margaret Douglass, stand up. You are guilty of one of the vilest crimes that
ever disgraced society; and the jury have found you so. You have taught a
slave girl to read in the Bible. No enlightened society can exist where such
offences go unpunished. The Court, in your case, do not feel for you one
solitary ray of sympathy, and they will inflict on you the utmost penalty
of the law. In any other civilized country you would have paid the forfeit of
your crime with your life, and the Court have only to regret that such is not
the law in this country. The sentence for your offence is, that you be im-
prisoned one month in the county jail, and that you pay the costs of this
prosecution. Sheriff, remove the prisoner to jail.' On the publication of
these proceedings, the Doctors of Divinity preached each a sermon on the
necessity of obeying the laws; the *New York Observer* noticed with much
pious gladness a revival of religion on Dr. Smith's plantation in Georgia,
among his slaves; while the *Journal of Commerce* commended this political
preaching of the Doctors of Divinity because it favoured slavery. Let us do
nothing to offend our Southern brethren."

However, at first, we were highly delighted at the idea of having
gained permission to be absent for a few days; but when the thought
flashed across my wife's mind, that it was customary for travellers to
register their names in the visitors' book at hotels, as well as in the
clearance or Custom-house book at Charleston, South Carolina—it
made our spirits droop within us.

So, while sitting in our little room upon the verge of despair, all at
once my wife raised her head, and with a smile upon her face, which
was a moment before bathed in tears, said, "I think I have it!" I asked
what it was. She said, "I think I can make a poultice and bind up my

right hand in a sling, and with propriety ask the officers to register my name for me." I thought that would do.

It then occurred to her that the smoothness of her face might betray her; so she decided to make another poultice, and put it in a white handkerchief to be worn under the chin, up the cheeks, and to tie over the head. This nearly hid the expression of the countenance, as well as the beardless chin.

⌐The poultice is left off in the engraving, because the likeness could not have been taken well with it on. ⌐

My wife, knowing that she would be thrown a good deal into the company of gentlemen, fancied that she could get on better if she had something to go over the eyes; so I went to a shop and bought a pair of green spectacles.

This was in the evening. We sat up all night discussing the plan, and making preparations. Just before the time arrived, in the morning, for us to leave, I cut off my wife's hair square at the back of the head, and got her to dress in the disguise and stand out on the floor. I found that she made a most respectable looking gentleman.

My wife had no ambition whatever to assume this disguise, and would not have done so had it been possible to have obtained our liberty by more simple means; but we knew it was not customary in the South for ladies to travel with male servants; and therefore, notwithstanding my wife's fair complexion, it would have been a very difficult task for her to have come off as a free white lady, with me as her slave; in fact, her not being able to write would have made this quite impossible. We knew that no public conveyance would take us, or any other slave, as a passenger, without our master's consent. This consent could never be obtained to pass into a free State. My wife's being muffled in the poultices, &c., furnished a plausible excuse for avoiding general conversation, of which most Yankee travellers are passionately fond.

There are a large number of free negroes residing in the southern States; but in Georgia (and I believe in all the slave States,) every coloured person's complexion is *primâ facie* evidence of his being a slave; and the lowest villain in the country, should he be a white man, has the legal power to arrest, and question, in the most inquisitorial and insulting manner, any coloured person, male or female, that he may find at large, particularly at night and on Sundays, without a written pass, signed by the master or some one in authority; or stamped free papers, certifying that the person is the rightful owner of himself.

If the coloured person refuses to answer questions put to him, he may be beaten, and his defending himself against this attack makes him an outlaw, and if he be killed on the spot, the murderer will be exempted from all blame; but after the coloured person has answered the questions put to him, in a most humble and pointed manner, he may then be taken to prison; and should it turn out, after further examination, that he was caught where he had no permission or legal right to be, and that he has not given what they term a satisfactory account of himself, the master will have to pay a fine. On his refusing to do this, the poor slave may be legally and severely flogged by public officers. Should the prisoner prove to be a free man, he is most likely to be both whipped and fined.

The great majority of slaveholders hate this class of persons with a hatred that can only be equalled by the condemned spirits of the infernal regions. They have no mercy upon, nor sympathy for, any negro whom they cannot enslave. They say that God made the black man to be a slave for the white, and act as though they really believed that all free persons of colour are in open rebellion to a direct command from heaven, and that they (the whites) are God's chosen agents to pour out upon them unlimited vengeance. For instance, a Bill has been introduced in the Tennessee Legislature to prevent free negroes from travelling on the railroads in that State. It has passed the first reading. The bill provides that the President who shall permit a free negro to travel on any road within the jurisdiction of the State under his supervision shall pay a fine of 500 dollars; any conductor permitting a violation of the Act shall pay 250 dollars; provided such free negro is not under the control of a free white citizen of Tennessee, who will vouch for the character of said free negro in a penal bond of one thousand dollars. The State of Arkansas has passed a law to banish all free negroes from its bounds, and it came into effect on the 1st day of January, 1860. Every free negro found there after that date will be liable to be sold into slavery, the crime of freedom being unpardonable. The Missouri Senate has before it a bill providing that all free negroes above the age of eighteen years who shall be found in the State after September, 1860, shall be sold into slavery; and that all such negroes as shall enter the State after September, 1861, and remain there twenty-four hours, shall also be sold into slavery for ever. Mississippi, Kentucky, and Georgia, and in fact, I believe, all the slave States, are legislating in the same manner. Thus the slaveholders make it almost impossible for free persons of colour to get out of the slave States, in order that they may sell them into slavery if they don't go. If no white persons travelled upon railroads except those who could get some one to vouch for their character in a penal bond of one thousand dollars, the railroad companies would soon go to the "wall." Such mean legislation is too low for comment; therefore I leave the villainous acts to speak for themselves.

But the Dred Scott decision is the crowning act of infamous Yankee legislation. The Supreme Court, the highest tribunal of the Republic, composed of nine Judge Jeffries's, chosen both from the free and slave States, has decided that no coloured person, or persons of African extraction, can ever become a citizen of the United States, or have any rights which white men are bound to respect. That is to say, in the opinion of this Court, robbery, rape, and murder are not crimes when committed by a white upon a coloured person.

Judges who will sneak from their high and honourable position down into the lowest depths of human depravity, and scrape up a decision like this, are wholly unworthy the confidence of any people. I believe such men would, if they had the power, and were it to their temporal interest, sell their country's independence, and

barter away every man's birthright for a mess of pottage. Well may
Thomas Campbell say—

> "United States, your banner wears,
>   Two emblems,—one of fame;
> Alas, the other that it bears
>   Reminds us of your shame!
> The white man's liberty in types
>   Stands blazoned by your stars;
> But what's the meaning of your stripes?
>   They mean your Negro-scars."

When the time had arrived for us to start, we blew out the lights,
knelt down, and prayed to our Heavenly Father mercifully to assist
us, as he did his people of old, to escape from cruel bondage; and
we shall ever feel that God heard and answered our prayer. Had we
not been sustained by a kind, and I sometimes think special, providence, we could never have overcome the mountainous difficulties
which I am now about to describe.

After this we rose and stood for a few moments in breathless silence,—we were afraid that some one might have been about the cottage listening and watching our movements. So I took my wife by
the hand, stepped softly to the door, raised the latch, drew it open,
and peeped out. Though there were trees all around the house, yet
the foliage scarcely moved; in fact, everything appeared to be as still
as death. I then whispered to my wife, "Come, my dear, let us make
a desperate leap for liberty!" But poor thing, she shrank back, in a
state of trepidation. I turned and asked what was the matter; she
made no reply, but burst into violent sobs, and threw her head upon
my breast. This appeared to touch my very heart, it caused me to
enter into her feelings more fully than ever. We both saw the many
mountainous difficulties that rose one after the other before our
view, and knew far too well what our sad fate would have been, were
we caught and forced back into our slavish den. Therefore on my

wife's fully realizing the solemn fact that we had to take our lives, as it were, in our hands, and contest every inch of the thousand miles of slave territory over which we had to pass, it made her heart almost sink within her, and, had I known them at that time, I would have repeated the following encouraging lines, which may not be out of place here—

> "The hill, though high, I covet to ascend,
> The *difficulty will not me offend;*
> For I perceive the way to life lies here:
> Come, pluck up heart, let's neither faint nor fear;
> Better, though difficult, the right way to go,—
> Than wrong, though easy, where the end is woe."

However, the sobbing was soon over, and after a few moments of silent prayer she recovered her self-possession, and said, "Come, William, it is getting late, so now let us venture upon our perilous journey."

We then opened the door, and stepped as softly out as "moon-light upon the water." I locked the door with my own key, which I now have before me, and tiptoed across the yard into the street. I say tiptoed, because we were like persons near a tottering avalanche, afraid to move, or even breathe freely, for fear the sleeping tyrants should be aroused, and come down upon us with double vengeance, for daring to attempt to escape in the manner which we contemplated.

We shook hands, said farewell, and started in different directions for the railway station. I took the nearest possible way to the train, for fear I should be recognized by some one, and got into the negro car in which I knew I should have to ride; but my *master* (as I will now call my wife) took a longer way round, and only arrived there with the bulk of the passengers. He obtained a ticket for himself and one for his slave to Savannah, the first port, which was about two hundred miles off. My master then had the luggage stowed away, and stepped into one of the best carriages.

But just before the train moved off I peeped through the window, and, to my great astonishment, I saw the cabinet-maker with whom I had worked so long, on the platform. He stepped up to the ticket-seller, and asked some question, and then commenced looking rapidly through the passengers, and into the carriages. Fully believing that we were caught, I shrank into a corner, turned my face from the door, and expected in a moment to be dragged out. The cabinet-maker looked into my master's carriage, but did not know him in his new attire, and, as God would have it, before he reached mine the bell rang, and the train moved off.

I have heard since that the cabinet-maker had a presentiment that we were about to "make tracks for parts unknown;" but, not seeing me, his suspicions vanished, until he received the startling intelligence that we had arrived safely in a free State.

As soon as the train had left the platform, my master looked round in the carriage, and was terror-stricken to find a Mr. Cray — an old friend of my wife's master, who dined with the family the day before, and knew my wife from childhood — sitting on the same seat.

The doors of the American railway carriages are at the ends. The passengers walk up the aisle, and take seats on either side; and as my master was engaged in looking out of the window, he did not see who came in.

My master's first impression, after seeing Mr. Cray, was, that he was there for the purpose of securing him. However, my master thought it was not wise to give any information respecting himself, and for fear that Mr. Cray might draw him into conversation and recognise his voice, my master resolved to feign deafness as the only means of self-defence.

After a little while, Mr. Cray said to my master, "It is a very fine morning, sir." The latter took no notice, but kept looking out of the window. Mr. Cray soon repeated this remark, in a little louder tone, but my master remained as before. This indifference attracted the attention of the passengers near, one of whom laughed out. This, I suppose, annoyed the old gentleman; so he said, "I will make him hear;" and in a loud tone of voice repeated, "It is a very fine morning, sir."

My master turned his head, and with a polite bow said, "Yes," and commenced looking out of the window again.

One of the gentlemen remarked that it was a very great deprivation to be deaf. "Yes," replied Mr. Cray, "and I shall not trouble that fellow any more." This enabled my master to breathe a little easier, and to feel that Mr. Cray was not his pursuer after all.

The gentlemen then turned the conversation upon the three great topics of discussion in first-class circles in Georgia, namely, Niggers, Cotton, and the Abolitionists.

My master had often heard of abolitionists, but in such a connection as to cause him to think that they were a fearful kind of wild animal. But he was highly delighted to learn, from the gentlemen's conversation, that the abolitionists were persons who were opposed to oppression; and therefore, in his opinion, not the lowest, but the very highest, of God's creatures.

Without the slightest objection on my master's part, the gentlemen left the carriage at Gordon, for Milledgeville (the capital of the State).

We arrived at Savannah early in the evening, and got into an omnibus, which stopped at the hotel for the passengers to take tea. I stepped into the house and brought my master something on a tray to the omnibus, which took us in due time to the steamer, which was bound for Charleston, South Carolina.

Soon after going on board, my master turned in; and as the captain and some of the passengers seemed to think this strange, and also questioned me respecting him, my master thought I had better get out the flannels and opodeldoc which we had prepared for the rheumatism, warm them quickly by the stove in the gentleman's saloon, and bring them to his berth. We did this as an excuse for my master's retiring to bed so early.

While at the stove one of the passengers said to me, "Buck, what have you got there?" "Opodeldoc, sir," I replied. "I should think it's opo-*devil*," said a lanky swell, who was leaning back in a chair with his heels upon the back of another, and chewing tobacco as if for a wager; "it stinks enough to kill or cure twenty men. Away with it, or I reckon I will throw it overboard!"

It was by this time warm enough, so I took it to my master's berth, remained there a little while, and then went on deck and asked the steward where I was to sleep. He said there was no place provided for coloured passengers, whether slave or free. So I paced the deck till a late hour, then mounted some cotton bags, in a warm place near the funnel, sat there till morning, and then went and assisted my master to get ready for breakfast.

He was seated at the right hand of the captain, who, together with all the passengers, inquired very kindly after his health. As my master had one hand in a sling, it was my duty to carve his food. But when I went out the captain said, "You have a very attentive boy, sir; but you had better watch him like a hawk when you get on to the North. He seems all very well here, but he may act quite differently there. I know several gentlemen who have lost their valuable niggers among them d——d cut-throat abolitionists."

Before my master could speak, a rough slave-dealer, who was sitting opposite, with both elbows on the table, and with a large piece of broiled fowl in his fingers, shook his head with emphasis, and in a deep Yankee tone, forced through his crowded mouth the words, "Sound doctrine, captain, very sound." He then dropped the chicken into the plate, leant back, placed his thumbs in the armholes of his fancy waistcoat, and continued, "I would not take a nigger to the North under no consideration. I have had a deal to do with niggers in my time, but I never saw one who ever had his heel upon free soil that was worth a d——n." "Now stranger," addressing my master, "if you have made up your mind to sell that ere nigger, I am your man; just mention your price, and if it isn't out of the way, I will pay for him on this board with hard silver dollars." This hard-featured, bristly-bearded, wire-headed, red-eyed monster, staring at my master as the serpent did at Eve, said, "What do you say, stranger?" He replied, "I don't wish to sell, sir; I cannot get on well without him."

"You will have to get on without him if you take him to the North," continued this man; "for I can tell ye, stranger, as a friend, I am an older cove than you, I have seen lots of this ere world, and I reckon I have had more dealings with niggers than any man living or dead. I was once employed by General Wade Hampton, for ten years, in doing nothing but breaking 'em in; and everybody knows that the General would not have a man that didn't understand his business. So I tell ye, stranger, again, you had better sell, and let me take him down to Orleans. He will do you no good if you take him across Mason's and Dixon's line; he is a keen nigger, and I can see from the cut of his eye that he is certain to run away." My master said, "I think not, sir; I have great confidence in his fidelity." "Fidevil," indignantly said the dealer, as his fist came down upon the edge of the saucer and upset a cup of hot coffee in a gentleman's lap. (As the scalded man jumped up the trader quietly said, "Don't disturb yourself, neighbour; accidents will happen in the best of families.") "It always makes me mad to hear a man talking about fidelity in niggers. There isn't a d——d one on 'em who wouldn't cut sticks, if he had half a chance."

By this time we were near Charleston; my master thanked the captain for his advice, and they all withdrew and went on deck, where the trader fancied he became quite eloquent. He drew a crowd around him, and with emphasis said, "Cap'en, if I was the President of this mighty United States of America, the greatest and freest country under the whole universe, I would never let no man, I don't care who he is, take a nigger into the North and bring him back here, filled to the brim, as he is sure to be, with d——d abolition vices, to taint all quiet niggers with the hellish spirit of running away. These air, cap'en, my flat-footed, every day, right up and down sentiments, and as this is a free country, cap'en, I don't care who hears 'em; for I am a Southern man, every inch on me to the backbone." "Good!" said an insignificant-looking individual of the slave-dealer stamp. "Three cheers for John C. Calhoun and the whole fair sunny South!" added the trader. So off went their hats, and out burst a terrific roar of irregular but continued cheering. My master took no more notice of the dealer. He merely said to the captain that the air on deck was too keen for him, and he would therefore return to the cabin.

While the trader was in the zenith of his eloquence, he might as well have said, as one of his kit did, at a great Filibustering meeting, that "When the great American Eagle gets one of his mighty claws upon Canada and the other into South America, and his glorious and starry wings of liberty extending from the Atlantic to the Pacific, oh! then, where will England be, ye gentlemen? I tell ye, she will only serve as a pocket-handkerchief for Jonathan to wipe his nose with."

On my master entering the cabin he found at the breakfast-table a young southern military officer, with whom he had travelled some distance the previous day.

After passing the usual compliments the conversation turned upon the old subject,—niggers.

The officer, who was also travelling with a man-servant, said to my master, "You will excuse me, Sir, for saying I think you are very likely to spoil your boy by saying 'thank you' to him. I assure you, sir, nothing spoils a slave so soon as saying, 'thank you' and 'if you please' to him. The only way to make a nigger toe the mark, and to keep him in his place, is to storm at him like thunder, and keep him trembling like a leaf. Don't you see, when I speak to my Ned, he darts like lightning; and if he didn't I'd skin him."

Just then the poor dejected slave came in, and the officer swore at him fearfully, merely to teach my master what he called the proper way to treat me.

After he had gone out to get his master's luggage ready, the officer said, "That is the way to speak to them. If every nigger was drilled in this manner, they would be as humble as dogs, and never dare to run away."

The gentleman urged my master not to go to the North for the restoration of his health, but to visit the Warm Springs in Arkansas.

My master said, he thought the air of Philadelphia would suit his complaint best; and, not only so, he thought he could get better advice there.

The boat had now reached the wharf. The officer wished my master a safe and pleasant journey, and left the saloon.

There were a large number of persons on the quay waiting the arrival of the steamer: but we were afraid to venture out for fear that some one might recognize me; or that they had heard that we were gone, and had telegraphed to have us stopped. However, after remaining in the cabin till all the other passengers were gone, we had our luggage placed on a fly, and I took my master by the arm, and with a little difficulty he hobbled on shore, got in and drove off to the best hotel, which John C. Calhoun, and all the other great southern fire-eating statesmen, made their head-quarters while in Charleston.

On arriving at the house the landlord ran out and opened the door: but judging, from the poultices and green glasses, that my master was an invalid, he took him very tenderly by one arm and ordered his man to take the other.

My master then eased himself out, and with their assistance found no trouble in getting up the steps into the hotel. The proprietor made me stand on one side, while he paid my master the attention and homage he thought a gentleman of his high position merited.

My master asked for a bed-room. The servant was ordered to show a good one, into which we helped him. The servant returned. My master then handed me the bandages, I took them downstairs in great haste, and told the landlord my master wanted two hot poultices as quickly as possible. He rang the bell, the servant came in, to whom he said, "Run to the kitchen and tell the cook to make two hot poultices right off, for there is a gentleman upstairs very badly off indeed!"

In a few minutes the smoking poultices were brought in. I placed them in white handkerchiefs, and hurried upstairs, went into my master's apartment, shut the door, and laid them on the mantel-piece. As he was alone for a little while, he thought he could rest a great deal better with the poultices off. However, it was necessary to have them to complete the remainder of the journey. I then ordered dinner, and took my master's boots out to polish them. While doing so I entered into conversation with one of the slaves. I may state here, that on the sea-coast of South Carolina and Georgia the slaves speak worse English than in any other part of the country. This is owing to the frequent importation, or smuggling in, of Africans, who mingle with the natives. Consequently the language cannot properly be called English or African, but a corruption of the two.

The shrewd son of African parents to whom I referred said to me, "Say, brudder, way you come from, and which side you goin day wid dat ar little don up buckra" (white man)?

I replied, "To Philadelphia."

"What!" he exclaimed, with astonishment, "to Philumadelphy?"

"Yes," I said.

"By squash! I wish I was going wid you! I hears um say dat dare's no slaves way over in dem parts; is um so?"

I quietly said, "I have heard the same thing."

"Well," continued he, as he threw down the boot and brush, and, placing his hands in his pockets, strutted across the floor with an air of independence—"Gorra Mighty, dem is de parts for Pompey; and I hope when you get dare you will stay, and nebber follow dat buckra back to dis hot quarter no more, let him be eber so good."

I thanked him; and just as I took the boots up and started off, he caught my hand between his two, and gave it a hearty shake, and, with tears streaming down his cheeks, said:—

"God bless you, broder, and may de Lord be wid you. When you gets de freedom, and sitin under your own wine and fig-tree, don't forget to pray for poor Pompey."

I was afraid to say much to him, but I shall never forget his earnest request, nor fail to do what little I can to release the millions of un-happy bondmen, of whom he was one.

At the proper time my master had the poultices placed on, came down, and seated himself at a table in a very brilliant dining-room, to have his dinner. I had to have something at the same time, in order to be ready for the boat; so they gave me my dinner in an old broken plate, with a rusty knife and fork, and said, "Here, boy, you go in the kitchen." I took it and went out, but did not stay more than a few minutes, because I was in a great hurry to get back to see how the invalid was getting on. On arriving I found two or three servants waiting on him; but as he did not feel able to make a very hearty dinner, he soon finished, paid the bill, and gave the servants each a trifle, which caused one of them to say to me, "Your massa is a big bug"—meaning a gentleman of distinction—"he is the greatest gentleman dat has been dis way for dis six months." I said, "Yes, he is some pumpkins," meaning the same as "big bug."

When we left Macon, it was our intention to take a steamer at Charleston through to Philadelphia; but on arriving there we found that the vessels did not run during the winter, and I have no doubt it was well for us they did not; for on the very last voyage the steamer made that we intended to go by, a fugitive was discovered secreted on board, and sent back to slavery. However, as we had also heard of the Overland Mail Route, we were all right. So I ordered a fly to the door, had the luggage placed on; we got in, and drove down to the Custom-house Office, which was near the wharf where we had to obtain tickets, to take a steamer for Wilmington, North Carolina. When we reached the building, I helped my master into the office, which was crowded with passengers. He asked for a ticket for himself and one for his slave to Philadelphia. This caused the principal officer—a very mean-looking, cheese-coloured fellow, who was sitting there—to look up at us very suspiciously, and in a fierce tone of voice he said to me, "Boy, do you belong to that gentleman?" I quickly replied, "Yes, sir" (which was quite correct). The tickets were handed out, and as my master was paying for them the chief man said to him, "I wish you to register your name here, sir, and also the name of your nigger, and pay a dollar duty on him."

My master paid the dollar, and pointing to the hand that was in the poultice, requested the officer to register his name for him. This seemed to offend the "high-bred" South Carolinian. He jumped up, shaking his head; and, cramming his hands almost through the bottom of his trousers pockets, with a slave-bullying air, said, "I shan't do it."

This attracted the attention of all the passengers. Just then the young military officer with whom my master travelled and conversed on the steamer from Savannah stepped in, somewhat the worse for brandy; he shook hands with my master, and pretended to know all about him. He said, "I know his kin (friends) like a book;" and as the officer was known in Charleston, and was going to stop there with friends, the recognition was very much in my master's favor.

The captain of the steamer, a good-looking, jovial fellow, seeing that the gentleman appeared to know my master, and perhaps not wishing to lose us as passengers, said in an off-hand sailor-like manner, "I will register the gentleman's name, and take the responsibility upon myself." He asked my master's name. He said, "William Johnson." The names were put down, I think, "Mr. Johnson and slave." The captain said, "It's all right now, Mr. Johnson." He thanked him kindly, and the young officer begged my master to go with him, and have something to drink and a cigar; but as he had not acquired these accomplishments, he excused himself, and we went on board and came off to Wilmington, North Carolina. When the gentleman finds out his mistake, he will, I have no doubt, be careful in future not to pretend to have an intimate acquaintance with an entire stranger. During the voyage the captain said, "It was rather sharp shooting this morning, Mr. Johnson. It was not out of any disrespect to you, sir; but they make it a rule to be very strict at Charleston. I have known families to be detained there with their slaves till reliable information could be received respecting them. If they were not very careful, any d——d abolitionist might take off a lot of valuable niggers."

My master said, "I suppose so," and thanked him again for help-ing him over the difficulty.

We reached Wilmington the next morning, and took the train for Richmond, Virginia. I have stated that the American railway carriages (or cars, as they are called), are constructed differently to those in England. At one end of some of them, in the South, there is a little apartment with a couch on both sides for the convenience of families and invalids; and as they thought my master was very poorly, he was allowed to enter one of these apartments at Peters-burg, Virginia, where an old gentleman and two handsome young ladies, his daughters, also got in, and took seats in the same carriage. But before the train started, the gentleman stepped into my car, and questioned me respecting my master. He wished to know what was the matter with him, where he was from, and where he was going. I told him where he came from, and said that he was suffering from a complication of complaints, and was going to Philadelphia, where he thought he could get more suitable advice than in Georgia.

The gentleman said my master could obtain the very best advice in Philadelphia. Which turned out to be quite correct, though he did not receive it from physicians, but from kind abolitionists who understood his case much better. The gentleman also said, "I reckon your master's father hasn't any more such faithful and smart boys as you." "O, yes, sir, he has," I replied, "lots on 'em." Which was literally true. This seemed all he wished to know. He thanked me, gave me a ten-cent piece, and requested me to be attentive to my good master. I promised that I would do so, and have ever since en-deavoured to keep my pledge. During the gentleman's absence, the ladies and my master had a little cosy chat. But on his return, he said, "You seem to be very much afflicted, sir." "Yes, sir," replied the gentleman in the poultices. "What seems to be the matter with you, sir; may I be allowed to ask?" "Inflammatory rheumatism, sir." "Oh! that is very bad, sir," said the kind gentleman: "I can sympa-thise with you; for I know from bitter experience what the rheuma-tism is." If he did, he knew a good deal more than Mr. Johnson.

The gentleman thought my master would feel better if he would lie down and rest himself; and as he was anxious to avoid conversation, he at once acted upon this suggestion. The ladies politely rose, took their extra shawls, and made a nice pillow for the invalid's head. My master wore a fashionable cloth cloak, which they took and covered him comfortably on the couch. After he had been lying a little while the ladies, I suppose, thought he was asleep; so one of them gave a long sigh, and said, in a quiet fascinating tone, "Papa, he seems to be a very nice young gentleman." But before papa could speak, the other lady quickly said, "Oh! dear me, I never felt so much for a gentleman in my life!" To use an American expression, "they fell in love with the wrong chap."

After my master had been lying a little while he got up, the gentleman assisted him in getting on his cloak, the ladies took their shawls, and soon all were seated. They then insisted upon Mr. Johnson taking some of their refreshments, which of course he did, out of courtesy to the ladies. All went on enjoying themselves until they reached Richmond, where the ladies and their father left the train. But, before doing so, the good old Virginian gentleman, who appeared to be much pleased with my master, presented him with a recipe, which he said was a perfect cure for the inflammatory rheumatism. But the invalid not being able to read it, and fearing he should hold it upside down in pretending to do so, thanked the donor kindly, and placed it in his waistcoat pocket. My master's new friend also gave him his card, and requested him the next time he travelled that way to do him the kindness to call; adding, "I shall be pleased to see you, and so will my daughters." Mr. Johnson expressed his gratitude for the proffered hospitality, and said he should feel glad to call on his return. I have not the slightest doubt that he will fulfil the promise whenever that return takes place. After changing trains we went on a little beyond Fredericksburg, and took a steamer to Washington.

At Richmond, a stout elderly lady, whose whole demeanour indicated that she belonged (as Mrs. Stowe's Aunt Chloe expresses it) to one of the "firstest families," stepped into the carriage, and took a seat near my master. Seeing me passing quickly along the platform, she sprang up as if taken by a fit, and exclaimed, "Bless my soul! there goes my nigger, Ned!"

My master said, "No; that is my boy."

The lady paid no attention to this; she poked her head out of the window, and bawled to me, "You Ned, come to me, sir, you runaway rascal!"

On my looking round she drew her head in, and said to my master, "I beg your pardon, sir, I was sure it was my nigger; I never in my life saw two black pigs more alike than your boy and my Ned."

After the disappointed lady had resumed her seat, and the train had moved off, she closed her eyes, slightly raising her hands, and in a sanctified tone said to my master, "Oh! I hope, sir, your boy will not turn out to be so worthless as my Ned has. Oh! I was as kind to him as if he had been my own son. Oh! sir, it grieves me very much to think that after all I did for him he should go off without having any cause whatever."

"When did he leave you?" asked Mr. Johnson.

"About eighteen months ago, and I have never seen hair or hide of him since."

"Did he have a wife?" enquired a very respectable-looking young gentleman, who was sitting near my master and opposite to the lady.

"No, sir; not when he left, though he did have one a little before that. She was very unlike him; she was as good and as faithful a nigger as any one need wish to have. But, poor thing! she became so ill, that she was unable to do much work; so I thought it would be best to sell her, to go to New Orleans, where the climate is nice and warm."

"I suppose she was very glad to go South for the restoration of her health?" said the gentleman.

"No; she was not," replied the lady, "for niggers never know what is best for them. She took on a great deal about leaving Ned and the little nigger; but, as she was so weakly, I let her go."

"Was she good-looking?" asked the young passenger, who was evidently not of the same opinion as the talkative lady, and therefore wished her to tell all she knew.

"Yes; she was very handsome, and much whiter than I am; and therefore will have no trouble in getting another husband. I am sure I wish her well. I asked the speculator who bought her to sell her to a good master. Poor thing! she has my prayers, and I know she prays for me. She was a good Christian, and always used to pray for my soul. It was through her earliest prayers," continued the lady, "that I was first led to seek forgiveness of my sins, before I was converted at the great camp-meeting."

This caused the lady to snuffle and to draw from her pocket a richly embroidered handkerchief, and apply it to the corner of her eyes. But my master could not see that it was at all soiled.

The silence which prevailed for a few moments was broken by the gentleman's saying, "As your 'July' was such a very good girl, and had served you so faithfully before she lost her health, don't you think it would have been better to have emancipated her?"

"No, indeed I do not!" scornfully exclaimed the lady, as she impatiently crammed the fine handkerchief into a little work-bag. "I have no patience with people who set niggers at liberty. It is the very worst thing you can do for them. My dear husband just before he died willed all his niggers free. But I and all our friends knew very well that he was too good a man to have ever thought of doing such an unkind and foolish thing, had he been in his right mind, and, therefore we had the will altered as it should have been in the first place."

"Did you mean, madam," asked my master, "that willing the slaves free was unjust to yourself, or unkind to them?"

"I mean that it was decidedly unkind to the servants themselves. It always seems to me such a cruel thing to turn niggers loose to shift for themselves, when there are so many good masters to take care of them. As for myself," continued the considerate lady, "I thank the Lord my dear husband left me and my son well provided for. Therefore I care nothing for the niggers, on my own account, for they are a great deal more trouble than they are worth, I sometimes wish that there was not one of them in the world; for the ungrateful wretches are always running away. I have lost no less than ten since my poor husband died. It's ruinous, sir!"

"But as you are well provided for, I suppose you do not feel the loss very much," said the passenger.

"I don't feel it at all," haughtily continued the good soul; "but that is no reason why property should be squandered. If my son and myself had the money for those valuable niggers, just see what a great deal of good we could do for the poor, and in sending missionaries abroad to the poor heathen, who have never heard the name of our blessed Redeemer. My dear son who is a good Christian minister has advised me not to worry and send my soul to hell for the sake of niggers; but to sell every blessed one of them for what they will fetch, and go and live in peace with him in New York. This I have concluded to do. I have just been to Richmond and made arrangements with my agent to make clean work of the forty that are left."

"Your son being a good Christian minister," said the gentleman, "It's strange he did not advise you to let the poor negroes have their liberty and go North."

"It's not at all strange, sir; it's not at all strange. My son knows what's best for the niggers; he has always told me that they were much better off than the free niggers in the North. In fact, I don't believe there are any white labouring people in the world who are as well off as the slaves."

"You are quite mistaken, madam," said the young man. "For instance, my own widowed mother, before she died, emancipated all her slaves, and sent them to Ohio, where they are getting along well. I saw several of them last summer myself."

"Well," replied the lady, "freedom may do for your ma's niggers, but it will never do for mine; and, plague them, they shall never have it; that is the word, with the bark on it."

"If freedom will not do for your slaves," replied the passenger,

"I have no doubt your Ned and the other nine negroes will find out their mistake, and return to their old home."

"Blast them!" exclaimed the old lady, with great emphasis, "if I ever get them, I will cook their infernal hash, and tan their accursed black hides well for them! God forgive me," added the old soul, "the niggers will make me lose all my religion!"

By this time the lady had reached her destination. The gentleman got out at the next station beyond. As soon as she was gone, the young Southerner said to my master, "What a d——d shame it is for that old whining hypocritical humbug to cheat the poor negroes out of their liberty! If she has religion, may the devil prevent me from ever being converted!"

For the purpose of somewhat disguising myself, I bought and wore a very good second-hand white beaver, an article which I had never indulged in before. So just before we arrived at Washington, an uncouth planter, who had been watching me very closely, said to my master, "I reckon, stranger, you are 'spiling' that ere nigger of yourn, by letting him wear such a devilish fine hat. Just look at the quality on it; the President couldn't wear a better. I should just like to go and kick it overboard." His friend touched him, and said, "Don't speak so to a gentleman." "Why not?" exclaimed the fellow. He grated his short teeth, which appeared to be nearly worn away by the incessant chewing of tobacco, and said, "It always makes me itch all over, from head to toe, to get hold of every d——d nigger I see dressed like a white man. Washington is run away with *spiled* and free niggers. If I had my way I would sell every d——d rascal of 'em way down South, where the devil would be whipped out on 'em."

This man's fierce manner made my master feel rather nervous, and therefore he thought the less he said the better; so he walked off without making any reply. In a few minutes we were landed at Washington, where we took a conveyance and hurried off to the train for Baltimore.

We left our cottage on Wednesday morning, the 21st of December, 1848, and arrived at Baltimore, Saturday evening, the 24th (Christmas Eve). Baltimore was the last slave port of any note at which we stopped.

On arriving there we felt more anxious than ever, because we knew not what that last dark night would bring forth. It is true we were near the goal, but our poor hearts were still as if tossed at sea; and, as there was another great and dangerous bar to pass, we were afraid our liberties would be wrecked, and, like the ill-fated *Royal Charter,* go down for ever just off the place we longed to reach.

They are particularly watchful at Baltimore to prevent slaves from escaping into Pennsylvania, which is a free State. After I had seen my master into one of the best carriages, and was just about to step into mine, an officer, a full-blooded Yankee of the lower order, saw me. He came quickly up, and, tapping me on the shoulder, said in his unmistakable native twang, together with no little display of his authority, "Where are you going, boy?" "To Philadelphia, sir," I humbly replied. "Well, what are you going there for?" "I am travelling with my master, who is in the next carriage, sir." "Well, I calculate you had better get him out; and be mighty quick about it, because the train will soon be starting. It is against my rules to let any man take a slave past here, unless he can satisfy them in the office that he has a right to take him along."

The officer then passed on and left me standing upon the platform, with my anxious heart apparently palpitating in the throat. At first I scarcely knew which way to turn. But it soon occurred to me that the good God, who had been with us thus far, would not forsake us at the eleventh hour. So with renewed hope I stepped into my master's carriage, to inform him of the difficulty. I found him sitting at the farther end, quite alone. As soon as he looked up and saw me, he smiled. I also tried to wear a cheerful countenance, in order to break the shock of the sad news. I knew what made him smile. He was aware that if we were fortunate we should reach our destination at five o'clock the next morning, and this made it the more painful to communicate what the officer had said; but, as there was no time to lose, I went up to him and asked him how he felt. He said "Much better," and that he thanked God we were getting on so nicely. I then said we were not getting on quite so well as we had anticipated. He anxiously and quickly asked what was the matter. I told him. He started as if struck by lightning, and exclaimed, "Good Heavens! William, is it possible that we are, after all, doomed to hopeless bondage?" I could say nothing, my heart was too full to speak, for at first I did not know what to do. However we knew it would never do to turn back to the "City of Destruction," like Bunyan's Mistrust and Timorous, because they saw lions in the narrow way after ascending the hill Difficulty; but press on, like noble Christian and Hopeful, to the great city in which dwelt a few "shining ones." So, after a few moments, I did all I could to encourage my companion, and we stepped out and made for the office; but how or where my master obtained sufficient courage to face the tyrants who had power to blast all we held dear, heaven only knows! Queen Elizabeth could not have been more terror-stricken, on being forced to land at the traitors' gate leading to the Tower, than we were on entering that office. We felt that our very existence was at stake, and that we must either sink or swim. But, as God was our present and mighty helper in this as well as in all former trials, we were able to keep our heads up and press forwards.

On entering the room we found the principal man, to whom my master said, "Do you wish to see me, sir?" "Yes," said this eagle-eyed officer; and he added, "It is against our rules, sir, to allow any person to take a slave out of Baltimore into Philadelphia, unless he can satisfy us that he has a right to take him along." "Why is that?" asked my master, with more firmness than could be expected. "Because, sir," continued he, in a voice and manner that almost chilled our blood, "if we should suffer any gentleman to take a slave past here into Philadelphia; and should the gentleman with whom the slave might be travelling turn out not to be his rightful owner; and should the proper master come and prove that his slave escaped on our road, we shall have him to pay for; and, therefore, we cannot let any slave pass here without receiving security to show, and to satisfy us, that it is all right."

This conversation attracted the attention of the large number of bustling passengers. After the officer had finished, a few of them said, "Chit, chit, chit;" not because they thought we were slaves endeavouring to escape, but merely because they thought my master was a slaveholder and invalid gentleman, and therefore it was wrong to detain him. The officer, observing that the passengers sympathised with my master, asked him if he was not acquainted with some gentleman in Baltimore that he could get to endorse for him, to show that I was his property, and that he had a right to take me off. He said, "No;" and added, "I bought tickets in Charleston to pass us through to Philadelphia, and therefore you have no right to detain us here." "Well, sir," said the man, indignantly, "right or no right, we shan't let you go." These sharp words fell upon our anxious hearts like the crack of doom, and made us feel that hope only smiles to deceive.

For a few moments perfect silence prevailed. My master looked at me, and I at him, but neither of us dared to speak a word, for fear of making some blunder that would tend to our detection. We knew that the officers had power to throw us into prison, and if they had done so we must have been detected and driven back, like the vilest felons, to a life of slavery, which we dreaded far more than sudden death.

We felt as though we had come into deep waters and were about being overwhelmed, and that the slightest mistake would clip asunder the last brittle thread of hope by which we were suspended, and let us down for ever into the dark and horrible pit of misery and degradation from which we were straining every nerve to escape. While our hearts were crying lustily unto Him who is ever ready and able to save, the conductor of the train that we had just left stepped in. The officer asked if we came by the train with him from Washington; he said we did, and left the room. Just then the bell rang for the train to leave; and had it been the sudden shock of an earthquake it could not have given us a greater thrill. The sound of the bell caused every eye to flash with apparent interest, and to be more steadily fixed upon us than before. But, as God would have it, the officer all at once thrust his fingers through his hair, and in a state of great agitation said, "I really don't know what to do; I calculate it is all right." He then told the clerk to run and tell the conductor to "let this gentleman and slave pass;" adding, "As he is not well, it is a pity to stop him here. We will let him go." My master thanked him, and stepped out and hobbled across the platform as quickly as possible. I tumbled him unceremoniously into one of the best carriages, and leaped into mine just as the train was gliding off towards our happy destination.

We thought of this plan about four days before we left Macon; and as we had our daily employment to attend to, we only saw each other at night. So we sat up the four long nights talking over the plan and making preparations.

We had also been four days on the journey; and as we travelled night and day, we got but very limited opportunities for sleeping. I believe nothing in the world could have kept us awake so long but the intense excitement, produced by the fear of being retaken on the one hand, and the bright anticipation of liberty on the other.

We left Baltimore about eight o'clock in the evening; and not being aware of a stopping-place of any consequence between there and Philadelphia, and also knowing that if we were fortunate we should be in the latter place early the next morning, I thought I might indulge in a few minutes' sleep in the car; but I, like Bunyan's Christian in the arbour, went to sleep at the wrong time, and took too long a nap. So, when the train reached Havre de Grace, all the first-class passengers had to get out of the carriages and into a ferry-boat, to be ferried across the Susquehanna river, and take the train on the opposite side.

The road was constructed so as to be raised or lowered to suit the tide. So they rolled the luggage-vans on to the boat, and off on the other side; and as I was in one of the apartments adjoining a baggage-car, they considered it unnecessary to awaken me, and tumbled me over with the luggage. But when my master was asked to leave his seat, he found it very dark, and cold, and raining. He missed me for the first time on the journey. On all previous occasions, as soon as the train stopped, I was at hand to assist him. This caused many slaveholders to praise me very much: they said they had never before seen a slave so attentive to his master: and therefore my absence filled him with terror and confusion; the children of Israel could not have felt more troubled on arriving at the Red Sea. So he asked the conductor if he had seen anything of his slave. The man being somewhat of an abolitionist, and believing that my master was really a slaveholder, thought he would tease him a little respecting me. So he said, "No, sir; I haven't seen anything of him for some time: I have no doubt he has run away, and is in Philadelphia, free, long before now." My master knew that there was nothing in this; so he asked the conductor if he would please to see if he could find me. The man indignantly replied, "I am no slavehunter; and as far as I am concerned everybody must look after their own niggers." He went off and left the confused invalid to fancy whatever he felt inclined. My master at first thought I must have been kidnapped into slavery by some one, or left, or perhaps killed on the train. He also thought of stopping to see if he could hear anything of me, but he soon remembered that he had no money. That night all the money we had was consigned to my own pocket, because we thought, in case there were any pickpockets about, a slave's pocket would be the last one they would look for. However, hoping to meet me some day in a land of liberty, and as he had the tickets, he thought it best upon the whole to enter the boat and come off to Philadelphia, and endeavour to make his way alone in this cold and hollow world as best he could. The time was now up, so he went on board and came across with feelings that can be better imagined than described.

After the train had got fairly on the way to Philadelphia, the guard came into my car and gave me a violent shake, and bawled out at the same time, "Boy, wake up!" I started, almost frightened out of my wits. He said, "Your master is scared half to death about you." That frightened me still more—I thought they had found him out; so I anxiously inquired what was the matter. The guard said, "He thinks you have run away from him." This made me feel quite at ease. I said, "No, sir; I am satisfied my good master doesn't think that." So off I started to see him. He had been fearfully nervous, but on seeing me he at once felt much better. He merely wished to know what had become of me.

On returning to my seat, I found the conductor and two or three other persons amusing themselves very much respecting my running away. So the guard said, "Boy, what did your master want?"* I replied, "He merely wished to know what had become of me." "No," said the man, "that was not it; he thought you had taken French leave, for parts unknown. I never saw a fellow so badly scared about losing his slave in my life. "Now," continued the guard, "let me give you a little friendly advice. When you get to Philadelphia, run away and leave that cripple, and have your liberty." "No, sir," I indifferently replied, "I can't promise to do that." "Why not?" said the conductor, evidently much surprised; "don't you want your liberty?" "Yes, sir," I replied; "but I shall never run away from such a good master as I have at present."

One of the men said to the guard, "Let him alone; I guess he will open his eyes when he gets to Philadelphia, and see things in another light." After giving me a good deal of information, which I afterwards found to be very useful, they left me alone.

I also met with a coloured gentleman on this train, who recommended me to a boarding-house that was kept by an abolitionist, where he thought I would be quite safe, if I wished to run away from my master. I thanked him kindly, but of course did not let him know

---

*I may state here that every man slave is called boy till he is very old, then the more respectable slaveholders call him uncle. The women are all girls till they are aged, then they are called aunts. This is the reason why Mrs. Stowe calls her characters Uncle Tom, Aunt Chloe, Uncle Tiff, &c.

who we were. Late at night, or rather early in the morning, I heard a fearful whistling of the steam-engine; so I opened the window and looked out, and saw a large number of flickering lights in the distance, and heard a passenger in the next carriage—who also had his head out of the window—say to his companion, "Wake up, old horse, we are at Philadelphia!"

The sight of those lights and that announcement made me feel almost as happy as Bunyan's Christian must have felt when he first caught sight of the cross. I, like him, felt that the straps that bound the heavy burden to my back began to pop, and the load to roll off. I also looked, and looked again, for it appeared very wonderful to me how the mere sight of our first city of refuge should have all at once made my hitherto sad and heavy heart become so light and happy. As the train speeded on, I rejoiced and thanked God with all my heart and soul for his great kindness and tender mercy, in watching over us, and bringing us safely through.

As soon as the train had reached the platform, before it had fairly stopped, I hurried out of my carriage to my master, whom I got at once into a cab, placed the luggage on, jumped in myself, and we drove off to the boarding-house which was so kindly recommended to me. On leaving the station, my master—or rather my wife, as I may now say—who had from the commencement of the journey borne up in a manner that much surprised us both, grasped me by the hand, and said, "Thank God, William, we are safe!" and then burst into tears, leant upon me, and wept like a child. The reaction was fearful. So when we reached the house, she was in reality so weak and faint that she could scarcely stand alone. However, I got her into the apartments that were pointed out, and there we knelt down, on this Sabbath, and Christmas-day,—a day that will ever be memorable to us,—and poured out our heartfelt gratitude to God, for his goodness in enabling us to overcome so many perilous difficulties, in escaping out of the jaws of the wicked.

Ellen Craft, in her escape disguise
as an ailing white planter.
Reprinted from Wilbur H. Siebert,
*The Underground Railroad from
Slavery to Freedom* (New York:
MacMillan, 1898).

Repatriated American citizens William and Ellen Craft,
some years after their daring escape and sojourn in England.
Reprinted from William Still, *The Underground Rail Road*
(Philadelphia: Porter & Coates, 1872).

This scene of privation, exposure to the elements, and travel afoot
depicts the conditions under which most fugitive slaves, in
contrast to the Crafts, typically made their way to freedom.
Reprinted from Still, *The Underground Rail Road.*

Rev. Theodore Parker, a leading Boston
abolitionist and member of the city's
Vigilance Committee. Reprinted from
Siebert, *The Underground Railroad.*

CAUTION!!

COLORED PEOPLE
OF BOSTON, ONE & ALL,
You are hereby respectfully CAUTIONED and
advised, to avoid conversing with the
Watchmen and Police Officers
of Boston,
For since the recent ORDER OF THE MAYOR &
ALDERMEN, they are empowered to act as
KIDNAPPERS
AND
Slave Catchers,
And they have already been actually employed in
KIDNAPPING, CATCHING, AND KEEPING
SLAVES. Therefore, if you value your LIBERTY,
and the *Welfare of the Fugitives* among you, *Shun*
them in every possible manner, as so many *HOUNDS*
on the track of the most unfortunate of your race.
Keep a Sharp Look Out for
KIDNAPPERS, and have
TOP EYE open.
APRIL 24, 1851.

This poster, worded by Rev. Theodore Parker, warns both
fugitives and free blacks alike of possible cooperation between
Boston's law enforcement officials and the southern slave catchers
known to be about the city. Reprinted from Langston Hughes
et al., *A Pictorial History of African Americans,* 6th ed.
(New York: Crown Publishers, 1995).

Faneuil Hall, Boston, a Revolutionary War-era symbol of American
principles of freedom that became a popular meeting place of
New England abolitionists. Reprinted from Edmund V. Gillon Jr.,
Early Illustrations and Views of American Architecture
(New York: Dover, n.d.).

The port of Liverpool, England, where the Crafts disembarked after their Atlantic crossing. Site of one of the largest black communities in nineteenth-century Europe, Liverpool was considered by hundreds of fugitive slaves, not only from America, but also from the Caribbean, to be the first truly free soil upon which they set foot. Reprinted from Henry S. Young, *Bygone Liverpool* (Liverpool: H. Young, 1913), courtesy of Hargrett Rare Book and Manuscript Library, University of Georgia Libraries.

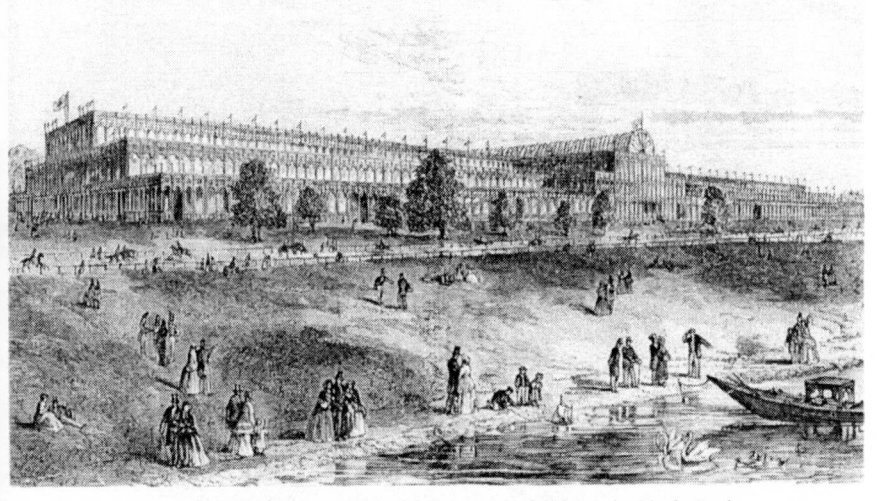

The Crystal Palace, home of the Great Exhibition in Hyde Park, London, and site of antislavery activities by the expatriated Crafts. Reprinted from John Clark Ridpath, *Ridpath's Universal History* (Cincinnati: Jones Brothers Pub. Co., n.d.).

Hiram Powers's *Greek Slave.*
Reprinted from Christopher
Hobhouse, *1851 and the Crystal
Palace* (New York: E. P. Dutton
& Co., Inc., n.d.).

Punch's "Virginian Slave."
Reproduced from *Punch* 20
(January–June 1851) with
permission of Punch, Ltd.

Part II

After my wife had a little recovered herself, she threw off the disguise and assumed her own apparel. We then stepped into the sitting-room, and asked to see the landlord. The man came in, but he seemed thunderstruck on finding a fugitive slave and his wife, instead of a "young cotton planter and his nigger." As his eyes travelled round the room, he said to me, "Where is your master?" I pointed him out. The man gravely replied, "I am not joking, I really wish to see your master." I pointed him out again, but at first he could not believe his eyes; he said "he knew that was not the gentleman that came with me."

But, after some conversation, we satisfied him that we were fugitive slaves, and had just escaped in the manner I have described. We asked him if he thought it would be safe for us to stop in Philadelphia. He said he thought not, but he would call in some persons who knew more about the laws than himself. He then went out, and kindly brought in several of the leading abolitionists of the city, who gave us a most hearty and friendly welcome amongst them. As it was in December, and also as we had just left a very warm climate, they advised us not to go to Canada as we had intended, but to settle at Boston in the United States. It is true that the constitution of the Republic has always guaranteed the slaveholders the right to come into any of the so-called free States, and take their fugitives back to southern Egypt. But through the untiring, uncompromising, and manly efforts of Mr. Garrison, Wendell Phillips, Theodore Parker, and a host of other noble abolitionists of Boston and the neighbourhood, public opinion in Massachusetts had become so much opposed to slavery and to kidnapping, that it was almost impossible for any one to take a fugitive slave out of that State.

So we took the advice of our good Philadelphia friends, and

settled at Boston. I shall have something to say about our sojourn there presently.

Among other friends we met with at Philadelphia, was Robert Purves, Esq., a well educated and wealthy coloured gentleman, who introduced us to Mr. Barkley Ivens, a member of the Society of Friends, and a noble and generous-hearted farmer, who lived at some distance in the country.

This good Samaritan at once invited us to go and stop quietly with his family, till my wife could somewhat recover from the fearful reaction of the past journey. We most gratefully accepted the invitation, and at the time appointed we took a steamer to a place up the Delaware river, where our new and dear friend met us with his snug little cart, and took us to his happy home. This was the first act of great and disinterested kindness we had ever received from a white person.

The gentleman was not of the fairest complexion, and therefore, as my wife was not in the room when I received the information respecting him and his anti-slavery character, she thought of course he was a quadroon like herself. But on arriving at the house, and finding out her mistake, she became more nervous and timid than ever.

As the cart came into the yard, the dear good old lady, and her three charming and affectionate daughters, all came to the door to meet us. We got out, and the gentleman said, "Go in, and make yourselves at home; I will see after the baggage." But my wife was afraid to approach them. She stopped in the yard, and said to me, "William, I thought we were coming among coloured people?" I replied, "It is all right; these are the same." "No," she said, "it is not all right, and I am not going to stop here; I have no confidence whatever in white people, they are only trying to get us back to slavery." She turned round and said, "I am going right off." The old lady then came out, with her sweet, soft, and winning smile, shook her heartily by the hand, and kindly said, "How art thou, my dear? We are all very glad to see thee and thy husband. Come in, to the fire; I dare say thou art cold and hungry after thy journey."

We went in, and the young ladies asked if she would like to go up-stairs and "fix" herself before tea. My wife said, "No, I thank you; I shall only stop a little while." "But where art thou going this cold night?" said Mr. Ivens, who had just stepped in. "I don't know," was the reply. "Well, then," he continued, "I think thou hadst better take off thy things and sit near the fire; tea will soon be ready." "Yes, come, Ellen," said Mrs. Ivens, "let me assist thee;" (as she commenced undoing my wife's bonnet-strings;) "don't be frightened, Ellen, I shall not hurt a single hair of thy head. We have heard with much pleasure of the marvellous escape of thee and thy husband, and deeply sympathise with thee in all that thou hast undergone. I don't wonder at thee, poor thing, being timid; but thou needs not fear us; we would as soon send one of our own daughters into slavery as thee; so thou mayest make thyself quite at ease!" These soft and soothing words fell like balm upon my wife's unstrung nerves, and melted her to tears; her fears and prejudices vanished, and from that day she has firmly believed that there are good and bad persons of every shade of complexion.

After seeing Sally Ann and Jacob, two coloured domestics, my wife felt quite at home. After partaking of what Mrs. Stowe's Mose and Pete called a "busting supper," the ladies wished to know whether we could read. On learning we could not, they said if we liked they would teach us. To this kind offer, of course, there was no objection. But we looked rather knowingly at each other, as much as to say that they would have rather a hard task to cram anything into our thick and matured skulls.

However, all hands set to and quickly cleared away the tea-things, and the ladies and their good brother brought out the spelling and copy books and slates, &c., and commenced with their new and green pupils. We had, by stratagem, learned the alphabet while in slavery, but not the writing characters; and, as we had been such a time learning so little, we at first felt that it was a waste of time for any one at our ages to undertake to learn to read and write. But, as the ladies were so anxious that we should learn, and so willing to teach us, we concluded to give our whole minds to the work, and see what could be done. By so doing, at the end of the three weeks we remained with the good family we could spell and write our names quite legibly. They all begged us to stop longer; but, as we were not safe in the State of Pennsylvania, and also as we wished to commence doing something for a livelihood, we did not remain.

When the time arrived for us to leave for Boston, it was like parting with our relatives. We have since met with many very kind and hospitable friends, both in America and England; but we have never been under a roof where we were made to feel more at home, or where the inmates took a deeper interest in our well-being, than Mr. Barkley Ivens and his dear family. May God ever bless them, and preserve each one from every reverse of fortune!

We finally, as I have stated, settled at Boston, where we remained nearly two years, I employed as cabinet-maker and furniture broker, and my wife at her needle; and, as our little earnings in slavery were not all spent on the journey, we were getting on very well, and would have made money, if we had not been compelled by the General Government, at the bidding of the slaveholders, to break up business, and fly from under the Stars and Stripes to save our liberties and our lives.

In 1850, Congress passed the Fugitive Slave Bill, an enactment too infamous to have been thought of or tolerated by any people in the world, except the unprincipled and tyrannical Yankees. The following are a few of the leading features of the above law; which requires, under heavy penalties, that the inhabitants of the *free* States should not only refuse food and shelter to a starving, hunted human being, but also should assist, if called upon by the authorities, to seize the unhappy fugitive and send him back to slavery.

In no case is a person's evidence admitted in Court, in defence of his liberty, when arrested under this law.

If the judge decides that the prisoner is a slave, he gets ten dollars; but if he sets him at liberty, he only receives five.

After the prisoner has been sentenced to slavery, he is handed over to the United States Marshal, who has the power, at the expense of the General Government, to summon a sufficient force to take the poor creature back to slavery, and to the lash, from which he fled.

Our old masters sent agents to Boston after us. They took out warrants, and placed them in the hands of the United States Marshal to execute. But the following letter from our highly esteemed and faithful friend, the Rev. Samuel May, of Boston, to our equally dear and much lamented friend, Dr. Estlin of Bristol, will show why we were not taken into custody.

> "*21, Cornhill, Boston,*
> "*November 6th, 1850.*

"My dear Mr. Estlin,

"I trust that in God's good providence this letter will be handed to you in safety by our good friends, William and Ellen Craft. They have lived amongst us about two years, and have proved themselves worthy, in all respects, of our confidence and regard. The laws of this republican and Christian land (tell it not in Moscow, nor in Constantinople) regard them only as slaves — chattels — personal property. But they nobly vindicated their title and right to freedom, two years since, by winning their way to it; at least, so they thought. But now, the slave power, with the aid of Daniel Webster and a band of lesser traitors, has enacted a law, which puts their dearly-bought liberties in the most imminent peril; holds out a strong temptation to every mercenary and unprincipled ruffian to become their kidnapper; and has stimulated the slaveholders generally to such desperate acts for the recovery of their fugitive property, as have never before been enacted in the history of this government.

"Within a fortnight, two fellows from Macon, Georgia, have been in Boston for the purpose of arresting our friends William and Ellen. A writ was served against them from the United States District Court; but it was not served by the United States Marshal; why not, is not certainly known: perhaps through fear, for a general feeling of indignation, and a cool determination not to allow this young couple to be taken from Boston into slavery, was aroused, and pervaded the city. It is understood that one of the judges told the Marshal that he would not be authorised in breaking the door of Craft's house. Craft kept himself close within the house, armed himself, and awaited with remarkable composure the event. Ellen, in the meantime, had been taken to a retired place out of the city. The Vigilance Committee (appointed at a late meeting in Fanueil Hall) enlarged their numbers, held an almost permanent session, and appointed various sub-committees to act in different ways. One of these committees called repeat-edly on Messrs. Hughes and Knight, the slave-catchers, and requested and advised them to leave the city. At first they peremptorily refused to do so, "'till they got hold of the niggers.' On complaint of different persons, these two fellows were several times arrested, carried before one of our county courts, and held to bail on charges of 'conspiracy to kidnap,' and of 'defa-mation,' in calling William and Ellen '*slaves.*' At length, they became so alarmed, that they left the city by an indirect route, evading the vigilance of many persons who were on the look-out for them. Hughes, at one time, was near losing his life at the hands of an infuriated coloured man. While these men remained in the city, a prominent whig gentleman sent word to William Craft, that if he would submit peaceably to an arrest, he and his wife should be bought from their owners, cost what it might. Craft replied, in effect, that he was in a measure the representative of all the other fugi-tives in Boston, some 200 or 300 in number; that, if he gave up, they would all be at the mercy of the slave-catchers, and must fly from the city at any sacrifice; and that, if his freedom could be bought for two cents, he would not consent to compromise the matter in such a way. This event has stirred up the slave spirit of the country, south and north; the United States gov-ernment is determined to try its hand in enforcing the Fugitive Slave law; and William and Ellen Craft would be prominent objects of the slavehold-ers' vengeance. Under these circumstances, it is the almost unanimous opinion of their best friends, that they should quit America as speedily as possible, and seek an asylum in England! Oh! shame, shame upon us, that Americans, whose fathers fought against Great Britain, in order to be FREE, should have to acknowledge this disgraceful fact! God gave us a fair and goodly heritage in this land, but man has cursed it with his devices and crimes against human souls and human rights. Is America the 'land of the free, and the home of the brave?' God knows it is not; and we know it too. A brave young man and a virtuous young woman must fly the American shores, and seek, under the shadow of the British throne, the enjoyment of 'life, liberty, and the pursuit of happiness.'

"But I must pursue my plain, sad story. All day long, I have been busy planning a safe way for William and Ellen to leave Boston. We dare not allow them to go on board a vessel, even in the port of Boston; for the writ is yet in the Marshal's hands, and he *may* be waiting an opportunity to serve it; so I am expecting to accompany them to-morrow to Portland, Maine, which is beyond the reach of the Marshal's authority; and there I hope to see them on board a British steamer.

"This letter is written to introduce them to you. I know your infirm health; but I am sure, if you were stretched on your bed in your last illness, and could lift your hand at all, you would extend it to welcome these poor hunted fellow-creatures. Henceforth, England is their nation and their home. It is with real regret for our personal loss in their departure, as well as burning shame for the land that is not worthy of them, that we send them away, or rather allow them to go. But, with all the resolute courage they have shown in a most trying hour, they themselves see it is the part of a foolhardy rashness to attempt to stay here longer.

"I must close; and with many renewed thanks for all your kind words and deeds towards us,

"I am, very respectfully yours,

"SAMUEL MAY, JUN."

Our old masters, having heard how their agents were treated at Boston, wrote to Mr. Filmore, who was then President of the States, to know what he could do to have us sent back to slavery. Mr. Filmore said that we should be returned. He gave instructions for military force to be sent to Boston to assist the officers in making the arrest. Therefore we, as well as our friends (among whom was George Thompson, Esq., late M.P. for the Tower Hamlets—the slave's long-tried, self-sacrificing friend, and eloquent advocate) thought it best, at any sacrifice, to leave the mock-free Republic, and come to a country where we and our dear little ones can be truly free.—"No one daring to molest or make us afraid." But, as the officers were watching every vessel that left the port to prevent us from escaping, we had to take the expensive and tedious overland route to Halifax.

We shall always cherish the deepest feelings of gratitude to the Vigilance Committee of Boston (upon which were many of the leading abolitionists), and also to our numerous friends, for the very kind and noble manner in which they assisted us to preserve our liberties and to escape from Boston, as it were like Lot from Sodom, to a place of refuge, and finally to this truly free and glorious country; where no tyrant, let his power be ever so absolute over his poor trembling victims at home, dare come and lay violent hands upon us or upon our dear little boys (who had the good fortune to be born upon British soil), and reduce us to the legal level of the beast that perisheth. Oh! may God bless the thousands of unflinching, disinterested abolitionists of America, who are labouring through evil as well as through good report, to cleanse their country's escutcheon from the foul and destructive blot of slavery, and to restore to every bondman his God-given rights; and may God ever smile upon England and upon England's good, much-beloved, and deservedly-honoured Queen, for the generous protection that is given to unfortunate refugees of every rank, and of every colour and clime.

On the passing of the Fugitive Slave Bill, the following learned doctors, as well as a host of lesser traitors, came out strongly in its defence.

The Rev. Dr. Gardiner Spring, an eminent Presbyterian Clergyman of New York, well known in this country by his religious publications, declared from the pulpit that, "if by one prayer he could liberate every slave in the world he would not dare to offer it."

The Rev. Dr. Joel Parker, of Philadelphia, in the course of a discussion on the nature of Slavery, says, "What, then, are the evils inseparable from slavery? There is not one that is not equally inseparable from depraved human nature in other lawful relations."

The Rev. Moses Stuart, D.D., (late Professor in the Theological College of Andover), in his vindication of this Bill, reminds his readers that "many Southern slaveholders are true *Christians.*" That "sending back a fugitive to them is not like restoring one to an idolatrous people." That "though we may *pity* the fugitive, yet the Mosaic Law does not authorize the rejection of the claims of the slaveholders to their stolen or strayed *property.*"

The Rev. Dr. Spencer, of Brooklyn, New York, has come forward in support of the "Fugitive Slave Bill," by publishing a sermon entitled the "Religious Duty of Obedience to the Laws," which has elicited the highest encomiums from Dr. Samuel H. Cox, the Presbyterian minister of Brooklyn (notorious both in this country and America for his sympathy with the slaveholder).

The Rev. W. M. Rogers, an orthodox minister of Boston, delivered a sermon in which he says, "When the slave asks me to stand between him and his master, what does he ask? He asks me to murder a nation's life; and I will not do it, because I have a conscience,—because there is a God." He proceeds to affirm that if resistance to the carrying out of the "Fugitive Slave Law" should lead the magistracy to call the citizens to arms, their duty was to obey and "if ordered to take human life, in the name of God to take it;" and he concludes by admonishing the fugitives to "hearken to the Word of God, and to count their own masters worthy of all honour."

The Rev. William Crowell, of Waterfield, State of Maine, printed a Thanksgiving Sermon of the same kind, in which he calls upon his hearers not to allow "excessive sympathies for a few hundred fugitives to blind them so as that they may risk increased suffering to the millions already in chains."

The Rev. Dr. Taylor, an Episcopal Clergyman of New Haven, Connecticut, made a speech at a Union Meeting, in which he deprecates the agitation on the law, and urges obedience to it; asking,—"Is that article in the Constitution contrary to the law of Nature, of nations, or to the will of God? Is it so? Is there a shadow of reason for saying it? I have not been able to discover it. Have I not shown you it is lawful to deliver up, in compliance with the laws, fugitive slaves, for the high, the great, the momentous interests of those [Southern] States?"

The Right Rev. Bishop Hopkins, of Vermont, in a Lecture at Lockport, says, "It was warranted by the Old Testament;" and inquires, "What effect had the Gospel in doing away with slavery? None whatever." Therefore he argues, as it is expressly permitted by the Bible, it does not in itself involve any sin; but that every Christian is authorised by the Divine Law to own slaves, provided they were not treated with unnecessary cruelty.

The Rev. Orville Dewey, D.D., of the Unitarian connexion, maintained in his lectures that the safety of the Union is not to be hazarded for the sake of the African race. He declares that, for his part, he would send his own brother or child into slavery, if needed to preserve the Union between the free and the slaveholding States; and, counselling the slave to similar magnanimity, thus exhorts him:—"*Your right to be free is not absolute, unqualified, irrespective of all consequences.* If my espousal of your claim is likely to involve your race and mine together in disasters infinitely greater than your personal servitude, then you ought not to be free. In such a case personal rights ought to be sacrificed to the general good. You yourself ought to see this, and be willing to suffer for a while — one for many."

If the Doctor is prepared, he is quite at liberty to sacrifice his "personal rights to the general good." But, as I have suffered a long time in slavery, it is hardly fair for the Doctor to advise me to go back. According to his showing, he ought rather to take my place. That would be practically carrying out his logic, as respects "suffering awhile — one for many."

In fact, so eager were they to prostrate themselves before the great idol of slavery, and, like Balaam, to curse instead of blessing the people whom God had brought out of bondage, that they in bringing up obsolete passages from the Old Testament to justify their downward course, overlooked, or would not see, the following verses, which show very clearly, according to the Doctor's own textbook, that the slaves have a right to run away, and that it is unscriptural for any one to send them back.

In the 23rd chapter of Deuteronomy, 15th and 16th verses, it is thus written:—"Thou shalt not deliver unto his master the servant which is escaped from his master unto thee. He shall dwell with thee, even among you, in that place which he shall choose in one of thy gates, where it liketh him best: thou shalt not oppress him."

"Hide the outcast. Betray not him that wandereth. Let mine outcasts dwell with thee. Be thou a covert to them from the face of the spoiler."—(Isa. xvi. 3, 4.)

The great majority of the American ministers are not content with uttering sentences similar to the above, or remaining wholly indifferent to the cries of the poor bondman; but they do all they can to blast the reputation, and to muzzle the mouths, of the few good men who dare to beseech the God of mercy "to loose the bonds of wickedness, to undo the heavy burdens, and let the oppressed go free." These reverend gentlemen pour a terrible cannonade upon "Jonah," for refusing to carry God's message against Nineveh, and tell us about the whale in which he was entombed; while they utterly overlook the existence of the whales which trouble their republican waters, and know not that they themselves are the "Jonahs" who threaten to sink their ship of state, by steering in an unrighteous direction. We are told that the whale vomited up the runaway prophet. This would not have seemed so strange, had it been one of the above lukewarm Doctors of Divinity whom he had swallowed; for even a whale might find such a morsel difficult of digestion.

> "I venerate the man whose heart is warm,
> Whose hands are pure; whose doctrines and whose life
> Coincident, exhibit lucid proof
> That he is honest in the sacred cause."

> "But grace abused brings forth the foulest deeds,
> As richest soil the most luxuriant weeds."

I must now leave the reverend gentlemen in the hands of Him who knows best how to deal with a recreant ministry.

I do not wish it to be understood that all the ministers of the States are of the Balaam stamp. There are those who are as uncompromising with slaveholders as Moses was with Pharaoh, and, like

Daniel, will never bow down before the great false God that has been set up.

On arriving at Portland, we found that the steamer we intended to take had run into a schooner the previous night, and was lying up for repairs; so we had to wait there, in fearful suspense, for two or three days. During this time, we had the honour of being the guest of the late and much lamented Daniel Oliver, Esq., one of the best and most hospitable men in the State. By simply fulfilling the Scripture injunction, to take in the stranger, &c., he ran the risk of incurring a penalty of 2,000 dollars, and twelve months' imprisonment.

But neither the Fugitive Slave Law, nor any other Satanic enactment, can ever drive the spirit of liberty and humanity out of such noble and generous-hearted men.

May God ever bless his dear widow, and eventually unite them in His courts above!

We finally got off to St. John's, New Brunswick, where we had to wait two days for the steamer that conveyed us to Windsor, Nova Scotia.

On going into a hotel at St. John's, we met the butler in the hall, to whom I said, "We wish to stop here to-night." He turned round, scratching his head, evidently much put about. But thinking that my wife was white, he replied, "We have plenty of room for the lady, but I don't know about yourself; we never take in coloured folks." "Oh, don't trouble about me," I said; "if you have room for the lady, that will do; so please have the luggage taken to a bed-room." Which was immediately done, and my wife went upstairs into the apartment.

After taking a little walk in the town, I returned, and asked to see the "lady." On being conducted to the little sitting-room, where she then was, I entered without knocking, much to the surprise of the whole house. The "lady" then rang the bell, and ordered dinner for two. "Dinner for two, mum!" exclaimed the waiter, as he backed out of the door. "Yes, for two," said my wife. In a little while the stout, red-nosed butler, whom we first met, knocked at the door. I called out, "Come in." On entering, he rolled his whisky eyes at me, and then at my wife, and said, in a very solemn tone, "Did you order dinner for two, mum?" "Yes, for two," my wife again replied. This confused the chubby butler more than ever; and, as the landlord was not in the house, he seemed at a loss what to do.

When dinner was ready, the maid came in and said, "Please, mum, the Missis wishes to know whether you will have dinner up now, or wait till your friend arrives?" "I will have it up at once, if you please." "Thank you, mum," continued the maid, and out she glided.

After a good deal of giggling in the passage, some one said, "You are in for it, butler, after all; so you had better make the best of a bad job." But before dinner was sent up, the landlord returned, and having heard from the steward of the steamer by which we came that we were bound for England, the proprietor's native country, he treated us in the most respectful manner.

At the above house, the boots (whose name I forget) was a fugitive slave, a very intelligent and active man, about forty-five years of age. Soon after his marriage, while in slavery, his bride was sold away from him, and he could never learn where the poor creature dwelt. So after remaining single for many years, both before and after his escape, and never expecting to see again, nor even to hear from, his long-lost partner, he finally married a woman at St. John's. But, poor fellow, as he was passing down the street one day, he met a woman; at the first glance they nearly recognized each other; they both turned round and stared, and unconsciously advanced, till she screamed and flew into his arms. Her first words were, "Dear, are you married?" On his answering in the affirmative, she shrank from his embrace, hung her head, and wept. A person who witnessed this meeting told me it was most affecting.

This couple knew nothing of each other's escape or whereabouts. The woman had escaped a few years before to the free States, by secreting herself in the hold of a vessel; but as they tried to get her back to bondage, she fled to New Brunswick for that protection which her native country was too mean to afford.

The man at once took his old wife to see his new one, who was also a fugitive slave, and as they all knew the workings of the infamous system of slavery, they could (as no one else can,) sympathise with each other's misfortune.

According to the rules of slavery, the man and his first wife were already divorced, but not morally; and therefore it was arranged between the three that he should live only with the lastly married wife, and allow the other one so much a week, as long as she requested his assistance.

After staying at St. John's two days, the steamer arrived, which took us to Windsor, where we found a coach bound for Halifax. Prejudice against colour forced me on the top in the rain. On arriving within about seven miles of the town, the coach broke down and was upset. I fell upon the big crotchety driver, whose head stuck in the mud; and as he "always objected to niggers riding inside with white folks," I was not particularly sorry to see him deeper in the mire than myself. All of us were scratched and bruised more or less. After the passengers had crawled out as best they could, we all set off, and paddled through the deep mud and cold and rain, to Halifax.

On leaving Boston, it was our intention to reach Halifax at least two or three days before the steamer from Boston touched there, *en route* for Liverpool; but, having been detained so long at Portland and St. John's, we had the misfortune to arrive at Halifax at dark, just two hours after the steamer had gone; consequently we had to wait there a fortnight, for the *Cambria*.

The coach was patched up, and reached Halifax with the luggage, soon after the passengers arrived. The only respectable hotel that was then in the town had suspended business, and was closed; so we went to the inn, opposite the market, where the coach stopped: a most miserable, dirty hole it was.

Knowing that we were still under the influence of the low Yankee prejudice, I sent my wife in with the other passengers, to engage a bed for herself and husband. I stopped outside in the rain till the coach came up. If I had gone in and asked for a bed they would have been quite full. But as they thought my wife was white, she had no difficulty in securing apartments, into which the luggage was afterwards carried. The landlady, observing that I took an interest in the baggage, became somewhat uneasy, and went into my wife's room, and said to her, "Do you know the dark man downstairs?" "Yes, he is my husband." "Oh! I mean the black man—the *nigger?*" "I quite understand you; he is my husband." "My God!" exclaimed the woman as she flounced out and banged to the door. On going upstairs, I heard what had taken place: but, as we were there, and did not mean to leave that night, we did not disturb ourselves. On our ordering tea, the landlady sent word back to say that we must take it in the kitchen, or in our bed-room, as she had no other room for "niggers." We replied that we were not particular, and that they could sent it up to our room,—which they did.

After the pro-slavery persons who were staying there heard that we were in, the whole house became agitated, and all sorts of oaths and fearful threats were heaped upon the "d——d niggers, for coming among white folks." Some of them said they would not stop there a minute if there was another house to go to.

The mistress came up the next morning to know how long we wished to stop. We said a fortnight. "Oh! dear me, it is impossible for us to accommodate you, and I think you had better go: you must understand, I have no prejudice myself; I think a good deal of the coloured people, and have always been their friend; but if you stop here we shall lose all our customers, which we can't do nohow." We said we were glad to hear that she had "no prejudice," and was such a staunch friend to the coloured people. We also informed her that we would be sorry for her "customers" to leave on our account; and as it was not our intention to interfere with anyone, it was foolish for them to be frightened away. However, if she would get us a comfortable place, we would be glad to leave. The landlady said she would go out and try. After spending the whole morning in canvassing the town, she came to our room and said, "I have been from one end of the place to the other, but everybody is full." Having a little foretaste of the vulgar prejudice of the town, we did not wonder at this result. However, the landlady gave me the address of some respectable coloured families, whom she thought, "under the circumstances," might be induced to take us. And, as we were not at all comfortable—being compelled to sit, eat and sleep, in the same small room—we were quite willing to change our quarters.

I called upon the Rev. Mr. Cannady, a truly goodhearted Christian man, who received us at a word; and both he and his kind lady treated us handsomely, and for a nominal charge.

My wife and myself were both unwell when we left Boston, and, having taken fresh cold on the journey to Halifax, we were laid up there under the doctor's care, nearly the whole fortnight. I had much worry about getting tickets, for they baffled us shamefully at the Cunard office. They at first said that they did not book till the steamer came; which was not the fact. When I called again, they said they knew the steamer would come full from Boston, and therefore we had "better try to get to Liverpool by other means." Other mean Yankee excuses were made; and it was not till an influential gentleman, to whom Mr. Francis Jackson, of Boston, kindly gave us a letter, went and rebuked them, that we were able to secure our tickets. So when we went on board my wife was very poorly, and was also so ill on the voyage that I did not believe she could live to see Liverpool.

However, I am thankful to say she arrived; and, after laying up at Liverpool very ill for two or three weeks, gradually recovered.

It was not until we stepped upon the shore at Liverpool that we were free from every slavish fear.

We raised our thankful hearts to Heaven, and could have knelt down, like the Neapolitan exiles, and kissed the soil; for we felt that from slavery

> "Heaven sure had kept this spot of earth uncurs'd,
> To show how all things were created first."

In a few days after we landed, the Rev. Francis Bishop and his lady came and invited us to be their guests; to whose unlimited kindness and watchful care my wife owes, in a great degree, her restoration to health.

We enclosed our letter from the Rev. Mr. May to Mr. Estlin, who at once wrote to invite us to his house at Bristol. On arriving there, both Mr. and Miss Estlin received us as cordially as did our first good Quaker friends in Pennsylvania. It grieves me much to have to mention that he is no more. Everyone who knew him can truthfully say —

> "Peace to the memory of a man of worth,
> A man of letters, and of manners too!
> Of manners sweet as Virtue always wears
> When gay Good-nature dresses her in smiles."

It was principally through the extreme kindness of Mr. Estlin, the Right Hon. Lady Noel Byron, Miss Harriet Martineau, Mrs. Reid, Miss Sturch, and a few other good friends, that my wife and myself were able to spend a short time at a school in this country, to acquire a little of that education which we were so shamefully deprived of while in the house of bondage. The school is under the supervision of the Misses Lushington, D.C.L. During our stay at the school we received the greatest attention from every one; and I am particularly indebted to Thomas Wilson, Esq., of Bradmore House, Chiswick, (who was then the master,) for the deep interest he took in trying to get me on in my studies. We shall ever fondly and gratefully cherish the memory of our endeared and departed friend, Mr. Estlin. We, as well as the Anti-Slavery cause, lost a good friend in him. However, if departed spirits in Heaven are conscious of the wickedness of this world, and are allowed to speak, he will never fail to plead in the presence of the angelic host, and before the great and just Judge, for downtrodden and outraged humanity.

"Therefore I cannot think thee wholly gone;
    The better part of thee is with us still;
Thy soul its hampering clay aside hath thrown,
    And only freer wrestles with the ill.

"Thou livest in the life of all good things;
    What words thou spak'st for Freedom shall not die;
Thou sleepest not, for now thy Love hath wings
    To soar where hence thy hope could hardly fly.

"And often, from that other world, on this
    Some gleams from great souls gone before may shine,
To shed on struggling hearts a clearer bliss,
    And clothe the Right with lustre more divine.

"Farewell! good man, good angel now! this hand
    Soon, like thine own, shall lose its cunning, too;
Soon shall this soul, like thine, bewildered stand,
    Then leap to thread the free unfathomed blue."

JAMES RUSSELL LOWELL

In the preceding pages I have not dwelt upon the great barbarities which are practised upon the slaves; because I wish to present the system in its mildest form, and to show that the "tender mercies of the wicked are cruel." But I do now, however, most solemnly declare, that a very large majority of the American slaves are overworked, under-fed, and frequently unmercifully flogged.

I have often seen slaves tortured in every conceivable manner. I have seen them hunted down and torn by bloodhounds. I have seen them shamefully beaten, and branded with hot irons. I have seen them hunted, and even burned alive at the stake, frequently for offences that would be applauded if committed by white persons for similar purposes.

In short, it is well known in England, if not all over the world, that the Americans, as a people, are notoriously mean and cruel towards all coloured persons, whether they are bond or free.

> "Oh, tyrant, thou who sleepest
> On a volcano, from whose pent-up wrath,
> Already some red flashes bursting up,
> Beware!"

SUPPLEMENTARY READINGS

Compiled and Introduced by Barbara McCaskill

Drawn from sources including journalism, fiction, drama, and correspondence, these excerpts underscore the events and issues discussed in the introduction to *Running a Thousand Miles for Freedom* and in the main text itself. The selections help to place the Crafts' story within its literary, cultural, and historical contexts and also give readers a sense of the complexity and scale of transatlantic abolitionism.

Notices of Blacks "Brought to Jail." *The Georgia Telegraph*
(19 December 1848).

Around the time the Crafts escaped to freedom, these notices were posted
in a Macon, Georgia, newspaper by Willis H. Hughes, one of the men who
would later travel to Boston to attempt to arrest the Crafts and return them
to slavery. Both notices, which describe age, height, skin color, and other
physical markers, show that the movements of blacks enslaved and free
were very restricted in the slaveholding states. Black men and women had
to verify permission to move abroad by producing passes signed by a master or guardian on demand of any white person. Posses of white vigilantes,
called "patrols," roamed the countryside day and night in order to waylay
runaways and other truant slaves. Detainees included bondmen or women
who had slipped from their homes temporarily to escape impending pun-
ishments or to visit friends and family, manumitted blacks who lacked free
papers or the patronage of a local white person, or those who had decided
to flee to the North, or to Canada or Mexico. Penalties for escaping varied
but were typically severe whippings or beatings, which also served as
deterrents for other slaves. Even pregnant women were not spared such
reprisals. To most slaveowners, however, preventive measures against escape and continuous surveillance for fugitives were far more preferable to
any permanent losses or damage to their valuable property. Such realities
emphasize the dangerous nature of the Crafts' decision to head north.

As a witty response to this oppression, Bostonians later described
Hughes and his companion, John Knight, as if they, too, were runaways.
The Vigilance Committee, assigned to protect the Crafts, composed a
poster alerting the citizenry that Hughes was "a short rowdyish looking fellow, about 5 feet 2, 35 to 40 years of age, sandy hair, red whiskers, black
short teeth, chews and smokes" and that Knight was "a tall, lank, lean looking fellow, 5 feet 10 or 11 inches, long dark hair, about 28 years old."

Brought to Jail.

By Alexander McGregor, about the 1st Sept., a girl by the name of Rose, about 50 years of age, who says she belongs to the estate of Bowers of Baldwin county, that she has been manumitted, and that Jerry Stone is her guardian. Her owner is requested to come forward, prove property, pay expenses, and take her away, or she will be dealt with as the law directs.

WILLIS H. HUGHES, Jailor Bibb County. Nov. 28th, 1848.

Brought to Jail.

A negro by the name of BOSON, about 50 years of age, five feet 5 or 6 inches high of very dark complexion, says he belongs to John Ward of Savannah. Also a man by the name of PETER, about twenty-five or thirty years of age, and says he belongs to James Bond of Lee county. The owners of said negroes are requested to come forward, [prove] property, pay charges and take them away, [or] they will be dealt with as the law directs.

WILLIS H. HUGHES, Jailor of Bibb co., oct. 10 – 8tf.

"William and Ellen Craft: Fugitives from Slavery."
The Non-Slaveholder 4.3 (March 1849): 69–70.

Almost instantaneous with their arrival on northern soil, very wide peri-
odical coverage of the Crafts' notorious escape was given on both sides of
the Atlantic and the Mason-Dixon Line. It is important to note how this
report stands as evidence of the reciprocity among fugitive slaves—in this
case, the Crafts and their amanuensis William Wells Brown. Note, for example, how the article introduces Brown as "himself a fugitive slave," as a
compatriot who has mutually suffered the very same indignities in bondage. Yet, on the other hand, Brown goes on to appear here as the wiser,
more capable mentor who has gained more experience than the novice
Crafts with curious Yankee audiences who are frequently hostile to talk of
abolition. The *Non-Slaveholder* (Philadelphia) reprints this story from the
National Anti-Slavery Standard (New York), and it quotes liberally from
the *Liberator* (Boston) and *Daily Mercury* (Newark). Therefore, this coverage is also an artifact of the cooperation among newspapers that might not
have shared a vision for achieving Emancipation, or even held similar opinions on the extent to which the freedmen and freedwomen could be inte-
grated into American society as citizens, voters, and policymakers. Be certain to note how the article from the *Daily Mercury,* which in the latter half
of this piece Brown is described as reading, comments on the themes of
blackness, whiteness, masculinity, and femininity that the narrative *Running* would later develop. The darkness assigned to William's complexion,
the "mysterious and unusual nature" of Ellen in her slaveholder's disguise,
William's "strapping" physique, and Ellen's "low womanly" voice—all
these identify the nineteenth century's discrete categories of race and sexuality, even as they reveal the ambiguity inherent in such classifications.

※

The singular and romantic story of the escape of these two persons from
slavery was told at the Annual Meeting of the Massachusetts Anti-Slavery

Society at Boston, week before last, by Wm. W. Brown, himself a fugitive slave, and the Crafts themselves appeared before the audience, exciting of course, a most lively interest by their appearance. The facts of their escape were stated by Mr. Brown, in a letter to the *Liberator* a few weeks since, and are briefly as follows:

"William and Ellen Craft, man and wife, lived with different masters in the State of Georgia. Ellen is so nearly white, that she can pass without suspicion for a white woman. Her husband is much darker. He is a mechanic, and by working nights and Sundays, he laid up money enough to bring himself and his wife out of slavery. Their plan was without precedent; and though novel, was the means of getting them their freedom. Ellen dressed in man's clothing, and passed as the *master,* while her husband passed as the *servant.* In this way they travelled from Georgia to Philadelphia. They are now out of the reach of the blood-hounds of the South. On their journey, they put up at the best hotels where they stopped. Neither of them can read or write. And Ellen, knowing that she would be called upon to write her name at the hotels, tied her right hand up as though it was lame, which proved of some service to her, as she was called upon several times at hotels to "register" her name. In Charleston, S.C., they put up at the hotel which Governor M'Duffie and John C. Calhoun generally make their home, yet these distinguished advocates of the "peculiar institution" say that the slaves cannot take care of themselves. They arrived in Philadelphia, in four days from the time they started. Their history, especially that of their escape, is replete with interest. They will be at the meeting of the Massachusetts Anti-Slavery Society, in Boston, in the latter part of this month, where I know the history of their escape will be listened to with great interest. They are very intelligent. They are young, Ellen 22, and William 24 years of age. Ellen is truly a heroine."

At the meeting in Boston W. W. Brown read an article from a Newark paper, (the *Daily Mercury*) which we copy as a most interesting part of the story. It is as follows:

An Incident at the South.

One bright starlight night in the month of December last, I found myself in the cabin of the steamer General Clinch, then lying in the port of Savannah, and bound for Charleston. I had gone early on board, in order to select a good berth, and having got tired of reading the papers, amused myself with watching the appearance of the passengers as they dropped in one after another, and I being a believer in physiognomy, forming my own opinions of their characters.

The second bell rang, and as I yawningly returned my watch to my pocket, my attention was attracted by the appearance of a young man who entered the cabin, supported by his servant, a strapping negro.

The man was bundled up in a capacious overcoat; his face was bandaged with a white handkerchief, and its expression entirely hid by a pair of enormous green spectacles.

There was something so mysterious and unusual about the young man, as he sat restlessly in the corner, that curiosity led me to observe him more closely.

He appeared anxious to avoid notice, and before the steamer had fairly left the wharf, requested in a low womanly voice to be shown to his berth, as he was an invalid and must retire early—his name he gave as Mr. Johnson. His servant was called and he was put quietly to bed. I paced the deck until Tybee light grew dim in the distance and then went to my berth.

I awoke in the morning with the sun shining in my face—we were then just passing St. Helena, and soon were out at sea. It was a mild, beautiful morning and most of the passengers were on deck enjoying the freshness of the air and stimulating their appetites for breakfast. Mr. Johnson soon made his appearance, arrayed the same as on the night before, and took his seat quietly on the guard of the boat.

From the better opportunity afforded by day light, I found that he was a slight built, apparently handsome young man, with black hair and eyes, and of a darkness of complexion that betokened Spanish extraction. Any notice from others seemed painful to him, so to satisfy my curiosity I questioned his servant who was standing near, and gained the following information.

His master was an invalid—he had suffered a long time with a complication of diseases that had baffled the skill of the best physicians in Georgia—he was now suffering principally with the "rheumatism," and was scarcely able to walk or help himself in any way. He came from Atlanta, Georgia, and was now on his way to Philadelphia, at which place resided an uncle a celebrated physician, through whose means he hoped to be restored to perfect health.

The information, communicated in a bold off hand manner, enlisted my sympathies for the sufferer, although it occurred to me that he walked rather too gingerly for a person afflicted with so many ailments.

We arrived at Charleston, and I there lost sight of Mr. Johnson, an acquaintance at my elbow remarking that he was either a *"woman* or a *genius."*

This morning I cut from the New York *Herald* the accompanying extract, and there is no doubt in my mind but that William and Ellen Craft are no other than my travelling companions, Mr. Johnson and servant.

Extract of a letter from William Farmer, Esq., of London,
to William Lloyd Garrison, 26 June 1851.
In *The Underground Rail Road*, by William Still.
Philadelphia: Porter and Coates, 1872. 374–77.

This letter, from the most comprehensive collection of stories of fugitive
slaves (Still was a black Underground Railroad conductor based in Philadelphia), is significant because it substantiates how the Crafts continued to
assume activist roles in the abolitionist movement, even during their exile
to Britain. Here, British abolitionist William Farmer, Esq., tells his American colleague William Lloyd Garrison of the Crafts' appearance in the
Crystal Palace ("the world's huge glass case") at the London World's Fair,
which was one of the most important spectacles of the nineteenth century.
In a kind of Olympics of commerce and progress, nations from throughout
the globe competed here to showcase their natural resources and manufactured consumer wares, furnishings, and conveniences. The irony that the
United States chose not to place its slaves on display was not lost on the
Crafts, especially since the centerpiece of the American exhibit, Hiram
Powers's sculpture *The Greek Slave,* had achieved a kind of cult status
among abolitionists. So, the Crafts determined to expose the one national
"product" which their native country seemed so reluctant to admit on the
world's great stage, even though the American exhibit was jammed with
cotton bales and other byproducts of the slaves' cultivation. Their decision
to promenade the American exhibition, each as a respectable member of
a middle-class, interracial couple—and on the day of the royal family's
visit—represents a brilliant manipulation of the public's interest in fugitives. The Crafts were now silently "talking back" to the culture which
had so very conscientiously muzzled the protests of chattel like them.
Both Powers's manacled *Greek Slave* and the "Virginian Slave" cartoon
from *Punch* that William Wells Brown affixed to it with a flourish became
mirrors that reflected the Crafts' intolerable position back to them and
their spectators.

Fortunately, we have, at the present moment, in the British Metropolis, some specimens of what were once American "chattels personal," in the persons of William and Ellen Craft, and William W. Brown, and their friends resolved that they should be exhibited under the world's huge glass case, in order that the world might form its opinion of the alleged mental inferiority of the African race, and their fitness or unfitness for freedom. A small party of anti-slavery friends was accordingly formed to accompany the fugitives through the Exhibition. . . . These ladies and gentlemen, together with myself, met at Mr. [George] Thompson's house, and, in company with Mrs. Thompson, and Miss Amelia Thompson, the Crafts and Brown, proceeded from thence to the Exhibition. Saturday was selected, as a day upon which the largest number of the aristocracy and wealthy classes attend the Crystal Palace, and the company was, on this occasion, the most distinguished that had been gathered together within its walls since its opening day. Some fifteen thousand, mostly of the upper classes, were there congregated, including the Queen, Prince Albert, and the royal children, the anti-slavery Duchess of Sutherland, (by whom the fugitives were evidently favorably regarded), the Duke of Wellington, the Bishops of Winchester and St. Asaph. . . .

In addition to the American exhibitors, it so happened that the American visitors were particularly numerous, among whom the experienced eyes of Brown and the Crafts enabled them to detect slave-holders by dozens. Mr. McDonnell escorted Mrs. Craft, and Mrs. Thompson; Miss Thompson, at her own request, took the arm of Wm. Wells Brown, whose companion she elected to be for the day; Wm. Craft walked with Miss Amelia Thompson and myself. This arrangement was purposely made in order that there might be no appearance of patronizing the fugitives, but that it might be shown that we regarded them as our equals, and honored them for their heroic escape from Slavery. Quite contrary to the feeling of ordinary visitors, the American department was our chief attraction. Upon arriving at Powers' "Greek Slave," our glorious anti-slavery friend, Punch's "Virginia Slave" was produced. I hope you have seen this production of our great humorous moralist. It is an admirably-drawn figure of a female slave in chains, with the inscription beneath, "The Virginia Slave, a companion for Powers' Greek Slave." The comparison of the two soon drew a small crowd, including several Americans, around and near us. Although they refrained from any audible expression of feeling, the object of the comparison was evidently understood and keenly felt. It would not have been prudent in us to have challenged, in words, an anti-slavery discussion in the World's Convention; but everything that we could with propriety do was done to induce them to break silence upon the subject. We had no intention, verbally, of taking the initiative in such a discussion; we confined ourselves to speaking at them, in order that they might be led to speak to us; but our efforts were of no avail. The gauntlet, which was unmistakably thrown down by our party, the Americans were too wary to take up. We spoke among each other of the wrongs of Slavery; it was in vain. We discoursed freely upon the iniquity of a professedly Christian Republic holding three millions of its population in cruel and degrading bondage; you might as well have preached to the winds. Wm. Wells Brown took "Punch's Virginia Slave" and deposited it within the enclosure by the "Greek Slave," saying audibly, "As an American fugitive slave, I place this 'Virginia Slave' by the side of the 'Greek Slave,' as its most fitting companion." Not a word, or reply, or remonstrance from Yankee or Southerner. We had not, however, proceeded many steps from the place before the "Virginia Slave" was removed. We returned to the statue, and stood near the American by whom it had been taken up, to give him an opportunity of making any remarks he chose upon the matter. Whatever were his feelings, his policy was to keep his lips closed. If he had felt that the act was wrongful, would he not have appealed to the sense of justice of the British bystanders, who are always ready to resist an insult offered to a foreigner in this country? If it was an insult, why not resent it, as became high-spirited Americans? But no; the chivalry of the South tamely allowed itself to be plucked by the beard; the garrulity of the North permitted itself to be silenced by three fugitive slaves. We promenaded the Exhibition between six and seven hours, and visited nearly every portion of the vast edifice. Among the thousands whom we met in our perambulations, who dreamed of any impropriety in a gentleman of character and standing, like Mr. McDonnell, walking arm-in-arm with a colored woman; or an elegant and accomplished young lady, like Miss Thompson, (daughter of the Hon. George Thompson, M. C.), becoming the promenading companion of a colored man? Did the English peers or peeresses? Not the most aristocratic among them. Did the representatives of any other country have their notions of impropriety shocked by the matter? None but Americans. To see the arm of a beautiful English young lady passed through that of "a nigger," taking ices and other refreshments with him, upon terms of the most perfect equality, certainly was enough to "rile," and evidently did "rile" the slave-holders who beheld it; but there was no help for it. Even the New York Broadway bullies would not have dared to utter a word of insult, much less lift a finger against Wm. Wells Brown, when walking with his fair companion in the World's Exhibition. It was a circumstance not to be forgotten by these Southern Bloodhounds. Probably, for the first time in their lives, they felt themselves thoroughly muzzled; they dared not even to bark, much less bite. Like the meanest curs, they had to sneak through the Crystal Palace, unnoticed and uncared for; while the victims who had been rescued from their jaws, were warmly greeted by visitors from all parts of the country. . . .

Brown and the Crafts have paid several other visits to the Great Exhibition, in one of which, Wm. Craft succeeded in getting some Southerners "out" upon the Fugitive Slave Bill, respecting which a discussion was held between them in the American department. Finding themselves worsted at every point, they were compelled to have recourse to lying, and unblushingly denied that the bill contained the provisions which Craft alleged it did. Craft took care to inform them who and what he was. He told them that there had been too much information upon that measure diffused in England for lying to conceal them. He has subsequently met the same parties, who, with contemptible hypocrisy, treated "the nigger" with great respect.

"How 'Aunt Nancy' Got Free."
The Pennsylvania Freeman 8:46 (13 November 1851): 1.

This narrative of a New Orleans servant who escaped by posing as a mammy illustrates that cross-dressing was not an unusual camouflage for individual slaves fleeing bondage. Indeed, it probably was a much more routine choice for individuals than for a couple like the Crafts, who ran away from servitude together with fictive identities. Still's *Underground Rail Road,* for example, includes detailed sketches from all over the Old South of men who left captivity disguised as women and women who escaped disguised as men. The transatlantic popularity of such stories (this one also appeared in the British *Anti-Slavery Advocate* and the Canadian *Voice of the Fugitive*) documents how, in spite of ostensibly rigid definitions of sexuality, nineteenth-century culture was fascinated by the spectacle of cross-dressing. Additionally, this article is meaningful because it represents the kind of popular antislavery material the Crafts would have most likely heard as regulars on the antislavery lecture circuit. They would have probably been given such stories as they learned to read and write, and certainly such pieces would have been available to inspire them as they developed their own narrative. For example, *Running* presents a community of black and white northerners who protect the Crafts from the slave-catchers and ease their transition into freedom. Similarly, this tale inserts a northern woman and her family with "no sympathy with slaveholding" into the company of such activists whose assistance was so crucial to the fugitives. Also prescient of *Running*—and exemplifying the suspenseful qualities of the slave-narrative genre—are the vignettes of close calls, one in which "Aunt Nancy" nearly misses the boat for her escape, and another when, as she boards the vessel, the captain almost has his suspicions of her true identity "aroused." Note, however, that "Aunt Nancy's" female disguise does not "unsex" his masculinity in the way that, as William tells us, Ellen's "habiliments of true manhood" threaten to divest her of her womanly ways.

☙❧

A merchant from the north, who was in the habit of visiting New Orleans every year for the purpose of buying cotton from a planter, became much attached to an old but interesting slave, who acted in the capacity of a house-servant. The merchant's wife, who sometimes accompanied her husband to the South, had no sympathy with slaveholding, and she therefore ventured one day, when the old and faithful slave was alone, to ask him if he would like to be free. His answer was, "Yes, Madam." Nothing more was said on the subject during a period of two years, in the course of which time the slave threw himself in the way of the good lady whenever an opportunity presented itself, hoping to hear her say something more to him about freedom. At length one day, when she saw him looking very earnestly at her, she asked him if he remembered the question that she had asked him about two years previous. The reply was, "Yes, Madam, I have thought of it more than a thousand times." He said that he wanted to be free, but knew not how he should obtain it. She then told him that if he would do as she directed him, that there was a chance for his freedom; when he joyfully replied that he would follow her directions. She told him that he must go to a certain store in the city every day at a certain hour if he could, where it would be made known to him what he should do to obtain his freedom. He attended accordingly at the time and place and was caused through a regular course of discipline to fit him for the enterprize. He was dressed in female attire and was commanded to answer to the name of Aunt Nancy. The lady would then put her infant child in the arms of Aunt Nancy, and make her take care of it. About half an hour was spent with Aunt Nancy in this way for several days, until she was fully initiated into the character she had to perform.

At length the time arrived when the merchant and his family were to return to the north on board of a certain steamboat. Aunt Nancy was notified to be at the store that morning about nine o'clock. It happened that morning that Aunt Nancy had so many little duties to perform that she was unable to keep her appointment until after nine o'clock, but, fortunately, from some cause or other, the boat in which they were to sail, did not get off until after ten o'clock. When the slave arrived at the store, they were anxiously waiting ready to dress him in female attire. They had also provided implements with which to shave him. His transformation being completed, and having put on a pair of lady's shoes, Aunt Nancy's protector told her to take the child and follow them to the boat. When they reached the boat the last bell was ringing.

After the gallant Captain had conducted the lady aboard, he offered his hand to Aunt Nancy to assist her in getting on board with the child; but the lady fearing that the Captain might have his suspicion aroused by the roughness of Aunt Nancy's hand and her masculine appearance, she told the Captain not to mind Aunt Nancy, as she could get on with the child alone. When they got snugly on board, a double state room was procured, a part of which Aunt Nancy was made to occupy with the child. The ladies on board appeared to think much of Aunt Nancy and the child. When they neared the mouth of the Ohio River, Aunt Nancy's apparel was changed, and she was transferred, in her proper costume, to another boat which was bound for St. Louis, the Captain of which was strictly bound to keep watch over her, under pain of forfeiture of her worth should she elude his vigilance, and to carefully deliver her into the keeping of a specified individual, all of which he agreed to do with fidelity. Arrived at St. Louis, she was duly handed over to the gentleman to whom she was consigned, and, by previous understanding, transferred into the hands of other friends; from them to others in Illinois, from whence by the spirit of freedom she was wafted to Canada, where she has donned, substantially and literally, the habiliments of true manhood as an independent freeman and thoroughgoing British subject.

Letter from Ellen Craft.
Anti-Slavery Advocate (December 1852): 22.

Ellen writes this spectacular open letter to the transatlantic antislavery press (also printed in the *Liberator, National Anti-Slavery Standard,* and *Pennsylvania Freeman*) in response to the rumor that she has tired of life in freedom and is arranging to return to Georgia escorted by an anonymous gentleman. This correspondence is a very important, rich example of how fugitive and free black women responded to pressures to conform to the norms of true womanhood (piety, purity, submission, domesticity), even as their lives demanded that they assume roles which did not fit the stereotypical model of middle-class white femininity. Ellen indicates that she is firmly ensconced in the socially acceptable roles of mother to a growing family and wife to a busy husband. However, her support of abolition demands that she step out of domesticity to occupy the role of female public speaker. And being in the spotlight was not for the timid. From Frances Ellen Watkins Harper to Maria W. Stewart to Sojourner Truth, nineteenth-century African American women speakers and commentators were heckled and even threatened with physical harm for unburdening their opinions before "promiscuous" or mixed-gender audiences. Or they were attacked for usurping what men claimed to be the masculine gender's rightful, exclusive, God-ordained position at the podium or in a byline. Ellen, however, boldly declares her intrinsic love of liberty and disdain of tyranny in order to make what would have been familiar abolitionist claims on behalf of the slave's humanity and entitlement to liberation. In this regard, her insouciant letter offers a counterpoint to how William in *Running* emphasizes her demureness and domesticity; and it alludes to how Ellen's life in England was marked by her transgressions of preconceived nineteenth-century notions of womanhood. She worked vigorously as a member of transatlantic abolition organizations; she gained employment as a teacher;

she raised the children while William traveled in Africa. Finally, be certain to note that Ellen's preference to "starve in England" anticipates the epigraph of *Running*, from the popular eighteenth-century abolitionist poet William Cowper, which expresses a similar sentiment.

꘍

In our last number, we mentioned that a strange report had gone the round of the slave states, to the effect that Ellen Craft had grown tired of liberty, and of the blessings of education in England, and had become so lost to self respect, that she had deserted her husband, and had placed herself under the protection of an American gentleman in London, on the express condition of his undertaking to restore her to that bondage from which she had so bravely emancipated herself. Of course, we did not believe this absurd calumny. Being personally acquainted with Mrs. Craft, we know that such a course was impossible to one with her keen perceptions of the monstrous injustice and cruelty of slavery. Although her experience has not been by any means of the worst, it has been tremendous. No woman of refined feelings and vigorous understanding, such as she possesses, could wish to return to the Southern States. However, to put the matter beyond doubt, we wrote directly to herself, and here is her answer:

Dear Sir:

I feel very much obliged to you for informing me of the erroneous report which has been so extensively circulated in the American newspapers. "That I had placed myself in the hands of an American gentleman in London, on condition that he would take me back to the family who held me as a slave in Georgia." So I write these few lines merely to say that the statement is entirely unfounded, for I have never had the slightest inclination whatever of returning to bondage; and God forbid that I should ever be so false to liberty as to prefer slavery in its stead. In fact, since my escape from slavery, I have gotten much better in every respect than I could have possibly anticipated. Though, had it been to the contrary, my feelings in regard to this would have been just the same, for I had much rather starve in

England, a free woman, than be a slave for the best man that ever breathed upon the American continent.

Yours very truly,

Ellen Craft

P.S. Mr. Craft joins me in kind regards to yourself and family.

We may well add, that since the above letter was written, this noble woman has become the happy mother of a freeborn child in the land where "no slave can breathe."

"The Fugitive Slave Bill and Its Effects." In *Five Hundred Thousand Strokes for Freedom, A Series of Anti-Slavery Tracts, of which Half a Million are Now First Issued by the Friends of the Negro*. Leeds Anti-Slavery Series, No. 32. 1853. Reprint, Miami: Mnemosyne, 1969. 1–12.

This tract is worth noting because it chronicles the dire impact of the Fugitive Slave Act of 1850 on former slaves such as William and Ellen Craft. It uses melodrama and sentiment to capture how the law resulted in the breakups of loving families and venerable community institutions, and how it created a dread among even freeborn blacks like Rachel Parker that was difficult for sympathetic whites to imagine. Make certain to observe how "A Scene in Boston," where Boston symbolizes both the Puritans' resistance to religious oppression and the Founding Fathers' commitment to inalienable human rights, is but a thinly veiled accusation that the nation has abandoned its Christian and revolutionary principles by upholding such legislation. Unlike *Running*, which presents Canada and the United Kingdom as more welcoming to the fugitive than the United States, this piece makes plain that "poverty and friendlessness," social ostracism, and emotional desolation often faced those runaways unceremoniously exiled to "a cold land of strangers." Attesting to the appeal of their own story, William and Ellen Craft were the subjects of the thirty-fifth tract in this series, which, like their narrative, was also distributed by William Tweedie.

⚥

In the autumn of 1850, the American Congress passed the Fugitive Slave Bill. Previously to the passing of that measure, the slave who could manage to escape from the Southern States found shelter and refuge in the North. There he was safe. Public opinion guarded him. Now the case is altered. The slave may be tracked, and claimed, and sent back to slavery. The bill denies the privilege of a trial by jury. By the law of the United States, a trial by jury is granted in all cases where the value in controversy exceeds twenty dollars. By the slave law this privilege is denied. "A human being," says Judge Jay, in commenting upon this law, "is stripped of every right, and reduced to the condition of a vendible beast of burden, with less ceremony and more celerity than one neighbour can recover of another the value of a pig in any court of justice."

The American Constitution declares that no person shall be deprived of life or property, without due process of law. Also, it provides, that in criminal prosecutions the accused shall enjoy a speedy and public trial by jury, and be confronted with the witnesses against him. The Fugitive Slave Bill sets aside these provisions, it suspends the Habeas Corpus Act. It makes an *ex parte* judgment of a court in one state conclusive against the alleged fugitive in the state where arrested; and not satisfied with this, no appeal from the decision of the commissioner of court is allowed. Besides this, as was said by the Hon. Horace Mann, the proofs which the law provides for, and declares *conclusive,* are abhorrent to reason, to common sense, and to the common law. It provides that evidence taken in a southern state, at any time or place which a claimant may select, without any notice or the possibility of knowledge on the part of the person to be robbed and enslaved by it, may be clandestinely carried or sent to any place where it is to be used, and there sprung upon its victim, as a wild beast springs from its jungle upon the passer-by; and it provides that this evidence, thus surreptitiously taken and used, shall be *conclusive proof* of the fact of slavery and of escape from slavery. It does not submit the sufficiency of the evidence to the judgment of the tribunal, but it arbitrarily makes it conclusive, whether sufficient or not. It abolishes the common law distinction between competency and credibility.

The cruel fruits of this law have been such as might be expected to grow on so wicked a stock. *The first man sent into slavery under it, Adam Gibson, was a free man.* When the claimant's agent brought Gibson to him, he refused to receive him, for he knew that all his household and neighbours would know that Gibson had never been his slave; and so, after this free man had been seized and sentenced as a slave, and dragged forcibly away from home to Maryland, as a slave, he was set adrift, and left to find his way back as best he could. Of the first *eight* persons doomed to slavery under this law, *four were free men.* In the case of Daniel, who was tried before

Mr. Commissioner Smith, at Buffalo, the slave-claimant never carried a single witness before the court that made the record of slavery and escape. In another case, in Philadelphia, Mr. Commissioner Ingraham decided some points directly against law and authority; and when a decision of a judge of the United States Court was produced against him, he coolly said he differed from the Judge, made out the certificate, pocketed the ten dollars, and sent a human being to bondage. And yet, with all these abominations, we find the Democratic Convention, which met at Baltimore last year, resolved to — "Abide by, and adhere to, a faithful execution of the Act known as the compromise measures settled by the last Congress — the Act for reclaiming from fugitive slaves service or labour, included." And further, that they — "Will resist all attempts at renewing, in Congress or out of it, the agitation of the slavery question, under whatever shape or colour the attempt may be made."

Nor were the Democrats alone; the Whigs at the same place agreed to a resolution almost equally infamous.

But we give an outline of the Bill. From that it will appear how it tramples on human rights, how it arms the slave-owner with terrible and irresponsible power, and deprives the slave of all chance of escape:—

"Marshals and deputies are required to execute all warrants and precepts, or other process, for the arrest and detention of fugitives, under penalty of a fine of 1000 dollars for the use of the claimant of such fugitive; and in case of the escape of such fugitive from the custody of a marshal, whether with or without his knowledge and connivance, the said marshal is to be liable to a prosecution for the full value of the said fugitive.

"Any person who shall knowingly hinder the arrest of a fugitive, or attempt to rescue him after arrest, or assist such fugitive, directly or indirectly, to escape, or harbour or conceal him, after notice or knowledge of the fact that he was a fugitive, shall be liable to a fine of 1000 dollars, and six months' imprisonment, by conviction before the proper district or territorial courts, and to a suit for damages of 1000 dollars for each fugitive lost to his owner by said obstruction or rescue, the same to be recovered by action of debt in any of the courts aforesaid."

Such are the provisions of the bill. Yet actually infamous as they are, President Fillmore, in the annual presidential message, could thus speak respecting it:—

"It is deeply to be regretted that, in several instances, officers of the Government, in attempting to execute the law for the return of fugitives from labour, have been openly resisted, and their efforts frustrated and defeated by lawless and violent mobs: that in one case such resistance resulted in the death of an estimable citizen, and in others serious injury ensued to those officers and to individuals who were using their endeavours to sustain the laws. Prosecutions have been instituted against the alleged offenders, so far as they could be identified, and are still pending. I have regarded it as my duty, in these cases, to give all aid legally in my power to the enforcement of the laws, and I shall continue to do so, wherever and whenever their execution may be resisted."

After this we cannot be surprised to find ministers of religion sanctioning the Fugitive Slave Bill.

It is supposed there are 50,000 fugitive slaves in the various free states of the Union. It is easy to imagine the terror which the passing of such a measure created. How families were broken up — churches disorganized — joy turned into mourning, and laughter into tears. We propose to illustrate the workings of this law. We have tales of misery enough to fill a volume — but we make a few selections. We will begin with — . . .

A Scene in Boston.

The following sketch exhibits the misery the Fugitive Slave Law produces by the disruption of social ties, and the annihilation of the domestic hearth:—

"A coloured girl, eighteen years of age, a few years ago escaped from slavery at the South. Through scenes of adventure and peril, almost more strange than fiction can create, she found her way to Boston. She obtained employment, secured friends, and became a consistent member of a Methodist church. She became interested in a very worthy young man of her own complexion, who was a member of the same church. They were soon married. Their home, though humble, was the abode of piety and contentment. Industrious, temperate, and frugal, all their wants were supplied. Seven years passed away. They had two little boys, one six and the other four years of age. These children, the sons of a free father, but of a mother who had been a slave, by the laws of our Southern states, were doomed to their mother's fate. These Boston boys, born beneath the shadow of Faneuil Hall, the sons of a free citizen of Boston, and educated in the Boston free schools, were, by the compromises of the Constitution, admitted to be slaves, the property of a South Carolinian planter. The Boston father had no right to his own sons. The law, however, had long been considered a dead letter. The Christian mother, as she morning and evening bowed with her children in prayer, felt that they were safe from the slave-hunter, surrounded as they were by the churches, the schools, and the free institutions of Massachusetts; but no — the Fugitive Slave Law was enacted, and the hopes of the slave-owners revived. A young, healthy, energetic mother, with two fine boys, was a rich prize. The poor woman was panic-struck. She was afraid to go out of doors, lest some from the South should see her. One day she recognised a man prowling, whom she knew came from the place from which she had fled. She was hid in a garret. Immediately after, the officer came with a writ for her arrest. It was a dark and stormy day. The rain, freezing as it fell, swept in floods through the streets of Boston. Night came, cold, black, and tempestuous. At midnight her friends took her in a hack, and conveyed her, with her children, to the house of her pastor. A prayer-meeting had been appointed there, at that hour, in behalf of their suffering sister. A small group of stricken hearts were there assembled. They knelt in prayer. The poor mother, thus hunted from her home, her husband far away, sobbed, in the bitterness of her anguish, as though her heart would break. Her little children, trembling before a doom, the enormity of which they were incapable of appreciating, cried loudly and uncontrollably. The humble minister caught the contagion. His voice became inarticulate through emotion. Bowing his head he ceased to pray, and yielded himself to the sobbings of sympathy and grief. After an hour of weeping, for the voice of prayer had passed away into the sublimity of unutterable anguish, they took this Christian mother and her children in a hack, and conveyed them to one of the Cunard steamers, which fortunately was to sail for Halifax the next day. They took them in the gloom of midnight, through the tempest-swept streets, lest the slave-hunter should meet them. Her brethren and sisters of the church raised a little money from their scanty means to pay her passage, and to save her, for a few days, from starving, after her first arrival in the cold land of strangers. Her husband soon returned to Boston, to find his home desolate, his wife and his children exiles in a foreign land."

From *Clotel; or, The President's Daughter:*
A Narrative of Slave Life in the United States,
by William Wells Brown.
London: Partridge and Oakey, 1853. 166–70.

This excerpt is significant as an example of the mutuality between Brown
and the Crafts. While William and Ellen certainly benefited from the experiences and lessons Brown shared with them, Brown, in turn, found in the
dramatic tale of their escape substantial grist for this work, his first novel.
In this scene of the fair-skinned slave Clotel's escape from slavery, Brown
makes little effort to hide the identity of his chapter's original source. He
includes numerous parallels to the Crafts' story: the quadroon Clotel's fellow fugitive is also named William, her disguise replicates Ellen's, her alias
of "Mr. Johnson" is also Ellen's, and she and William stay in John C. Calhoun's hotel, to name just a few. However, this section of the novel also
bears revisiting for the clues it offers to how an antislavery writer like
Brown fictionalized such well-known stories as that of the Crafts' escape.
He heightens the urgency of the fugitives' flight by setting Clotel and William's original meeting in Mississippi, which was considered by most abolitionists to be, like Louisiana, a death sentence for the slaves, where labors
were the hardest, the masters the crudest, and mortality rates the highest.
To add veracity to his story, he also borrows from the slave-narrative genre
its technique of including authenticating or corroborating documentation:
in this instance, the account from the southern papers that closes the
chapter.

※

We have seen Clotel sold to Mr. French in Vicksburg, her hair cut short,
and everything done to make her realise her position as a servant. Then we
have seen her re-sold, because her owners feared she would die through
grief. As yet her new purchaser treated her with respectful gentleness, and
sought to win her favour by flattery and presents, knowing that whatever

he gave her he could take back again. But she dreaded every moment lest the scene should change, and trembled at the sound of every footfall. At every interview with her new master Clotel stoutly maintained that she had left a husband in Virginia, and would never think of taking another. The gold watch and chain, and other glittering presents which he purchased for her, were all laid aside by the quadroon, as if they were of no value to her. In the same house with her was another servant, a man, who had from time to time hired himself from his master. William was his name. He could feel for Clotel, for he, like her, had been separated from near and dear relatives, and often tried to console the poor woman. One day the quadroon observed to him that her hair was growing out again. "Yes," replied William, "you look a good deal like a man with your short hair." "Oh," rejoined she, "I have often been told that I would make a better looking man than a woman. If I had the money," continued she, "I would bid farewell to this place." In a moment more she feared that she had said too much, and smilingly remarked, "I am always talking nonsense." William was a tall, full-bodied negro, whose very countenance beamed with intelligence. Being a mechanic, he had, by his own industry, made more than what he paid his owner; this he laid aside, with the hope that some day he might get enough to purchase his freedom. He had in his chest one hundred and fifty dollars. His was a heart that felt for others, and he had again and again wiped the tears from his eyes as he heard the story of Clotel as related by herself. "If she can get free with a little money, why not give her what I have?" thought he, and then he resolved to do it. An hour after, he came into the quadroon's room and laid the money in her lap, and said, "There, Miss Clotel, you said if you had the means you would leave this place; there is money enough to take you to England, where you will be free. You are much fairer than many of the white women of the South, and can easily pass for a free white lady." At first Clotel feared that it was a plan by which the negro wished to try her fidelity to her owner; but she was soon convinced by his earnest manner, and the deep feeling with which he spoke, that he was honest. "I will take the money only on one condition," said she; "and that is, that I effect your escape as well as my own." "How can that be done?" he inquired. "I will assume the disguise of a gentleman and you that of a servant, and we will take passage on a steamboat and go to Cincinnati, and thence to Canada." Here William put in several objections to the plan. He feared detection, and he well know that, when a slave is once caught when attempting to escape, if returned is sure to be worse treated than before. However, Clotel satisfied him that the plan could be carried out if he would only play his part.

The resolution was taken, the clothes for her disguise procured, and before night everything was in readiness for their departure. That night Mr. Cooper, their master, was to attend a party, and this was their opportunity. William went to the wharf to look out for a boat, and had scarcely reached the landing ere he heard the puffing of a steamer. He returned and reported the fact. Clotel had already packed her trunk, and had only to dress and all was ready. In less than an hour they were on board the boat. Under the assumed name of "Mr. Johnson," Clotel went to the clerk's office and took a private state room for herself, and paid her own and servant's fare. Besides being attired in a neat suit of black, she had a white silk handkerchief tied round her chin, as if she was an invalid. A pair of green glasses covered her eyes; and fearing that she would be talked to too much and thus render her liable to be detected, she assumed to be very ill. On the other hand, William was playing his part well in the servants' hall; he was talking loudly of his master's wealth. Nothing appeared as good on the boat as in his master's fine mansion. "I don't like dees steamboats no how," said William; "I hope when marser goes on a journey agin he will take de carriage and de hosses." Mr. Johnson (for such was the name by which Clotel now went) remained in his room, to avoid, as far as possible, conversation with others. After a passage of seven days they arrived at Louisville, and put up at Gough's Hotel. Here they had to await the departure of another boat for the North. They were now in their most critical position. They were still in a slave state, and John C. Calhoun, a distinguished slaveowner, was a guest at this hotel. They feared, also, that trouble would attend their attempt to leave this place for the North, as all persons taking negroes with them have to give bail that such negroes are not runaway slaves. The law upon this point is very stringent: all steamboats and other public conveyances are liable to a fine for every slave that escapes by them, besides paying the full value for the slave. After a delay of four hours, Mr. Johnson and servant took passage on the steamer Rodolph, for Pittsburgh. It is usual, before the departure of the boats, for an officer to examine every part of the vessel to see that no slave secretes himself on board. "Where are you going?" asked the officer of William, as he was doing his duty on this occasion. "I am going with marser," was the quick reply. "Who is your master?" "Mr. Johnson, sir, a gentleman in the cabin." "You must take him to the office and satisfy that captain that all is right, or you can't go on this boat." William informed his master what the officer had said. The boat was on the eve of going, and no time could be lost, yet they knew not what to do. At last they went to the office, and Mr. Johnson, addressing the captain, said, "I am informed that my boy can't go with me unless I give security that he belongs to me." "Yes," replied the captain, "that is the law." "A very strange law indeed," rejoined Mr. Johnson, "that one can't take his property with him." After a conversation of some minutes, and a plea on the part of Johnson that he did not wish to be delayed owing to his illness, they were permitted to take their passage without farther trouble, and the boat was soon on its way up the river. The fugitives had now passed the Rubicon, and the next place at which they would land would be in a Free State. Clotel called William to her room, and said to him, "We are now free, you can go on your way to Canada, and I shall go to Virginia in search of my daughter." The announcement that she was going to risk her liberty in a Slave State was unwelcome news to William. With all the eloquence he could command, he tried to persuade Clotel that she could not escape detection, and was only throwing her freedom away. But she had counted the cost, and made up her mind for the worst. In return for the money he had furnished, she had secured for him his liberty, and their engagement was at an end.

After a quick passage the fugitives arrived at Cincinnati, and there separated. William proceeded on his way to Canada, and Clotel again resumed her own apparel, and prepared to start in search of her child.

Attempt to kidnap Ellen and William Craft. From *The Trial of Theodore Parker, for the "Misdemeanor" of a Speech in Faneuil Hall against Kidnapping, before the Circuit Court of the United States at Boston, April 3, 1855.* Boston: For the author, 1855. 146–48.

Abolition's most charismatic speeches very often originated from the passionate debates that the Fugitive Slave Act of 1850 ignited. On 3 April 1855 the Unitarian minister Theodore Parker gave such a speech in Boston's Faneuil Hall; and, as a consequence, he landed in court facing a misdemeanor violation. What to find worth considering in this selection is not that the Crafts' story figures in it, but how it does. To underscore the cruelties of enslavement—and the ruthlessness of any law that would return ex-slaves to bondage—Parker tells the court that Ellen had to leave "the groans and moanings" of a dying child in order to serve her mistress. While she attended her mistress, her only baby passed away. Certainly, Parker is relying upon the sacred value placed on motherhood to arouse the indignation of the court against enslavement. Significant, however, is the absence of this scene in *Running*. Admitting to a child in slavery would have undermined the Crafts' romantic theme that they wanted their children all to be born free. Or, perhaps, the Crafts feared that readers would criticize Ellen for not being mother enough to disobey her mistress for the sake of comforting her child. Like all slave narratives, *Running* does not rely on authenticity at the expense of artistic license. And even in the twentieth century, writers would revisit the impact of the Fugitive Slave Act on American social history. In 1914, for example, Alice Dunbar-Nelson, who then was married to the poet Paul Laurence Dunbar, would include Charles Langston's 1859 speech, "Should Colored Men Be Subject to the Pains and Penalties of the Fugitive Slave Law?" in her *Masterpieces of Negro Eloquence*.

Gentlemen of the Jury, you know the story of William and Ellen Craft. They were slaves in Georgia; their master was said to be a "very pious man," "an excellent Christian." Ellen had a little baby,—it was sick and ready to die. But one day her "owner"—for this wife and mother was only a piece of property—had a dinner party at his house. Ellen must leave her dying child and wait upon the table. She was not permitted to catch the last sighing of her only child with her own lips; other and ruder hands must attend to the mother's sad privilege. But the groans and moanings of the dying child came to her ear and mingled with the joy and merriment of the guests whom the mother must wait upon. At length the moanings all were still—for Death took a North-side view of the little boy, and the born-slave had gone where the servant is free from his master and the weary is at rest— for there the wicked cease from troubling. Ellen and William resolved to flee to the North. They cherished the plan for years; he was a joiner, and hired himself of his owner for about two hundred dollars a year. They saved a little money, and stealthily, piece by piece, they bought a suit of gentleman's clothes to fit the wife; no two garments were obtained of the same dealer. Ellen disguised herself as a man, William attending as her servant, and so they fled off and came to Boston. No doubt these Hon. Judges think it was a very "immoral" thing. Mr. Curtis knows no morality here but "legality." Nay, it was a wicked thing—for Mr. Everett, a most accomplished scholar, and once a Unitarian minister, makes St. Paul command "Slaves, obey your masters!" Nay, Hon. Judge Sprague says it is a "precept" of our "Divine Master!"

Ellen and William lived here in Boston, intelligent, respected, happy. The first blow of the fugitive slave bill must fall on them. In October, 1850, one Hughes, a jailer from Macon, Georgia, a public negro-whipper, who had once beaten Ellen's uncle "almost to death," came here with one Knight, his attendant, to kidnap William and Ellen Craft. They applied to Hon. Mr. Hallett for a writ. Perhaps they had heard (false) rumors that the Hon. Commissioner was "a little slippery in his character;" that he was "not overscrupulous in his conduct;" that he "would do any dirty work for political preferment." Gentlemen, you know that such rumors will get abroad, and will be whispered of the best of men. Of course you would never believe them in this case: but a kidnapper from Georgia might; "distance lends" illusion, as well as "enchantment, to the view." But be that as

it may, Mr. Hallett (in 1850) appeared to have too much manhood to kidnap a man. He was better than his reputation; I mean his reputation with
Knight and Hughes, and would not (then) steal Mr. and Mrs. Craft. This
is small praise; it is large in comparison with the conduct of his official
brethren. But for the salvation of the Union another Commissioner was
found who had no such scruples. This Honorable Court—Mr. Woodbury
was then in the chief place, and Mr. Sprague in his present position—
issued the writ of man-stealing. Two gentlemen of this city were eminently,
but secretly, active in their attempt to kidnap their victim. I shall speak of
them by and by. Somebody took care of Ellen Craft. William less needed
help; he armed himself with pistols and a poignard, and walked in the
streets in the face of the sun. He was a tall, brave man, and was quite as cool
then as this Honorable Court is now, while I relate their "glorious first essay" in man-stealing. Public opinion at length drove the (southern) kidnappers from Boston. Then the Crafts also left the town and the country,
and found in the Monarchical Aristocracy of Old England what the New
England Democracy refused to allow them—protection of their unalien-
able right to Life, Liberty, and the pursuit of Happiness.

From *The Freedmen's Book*, by Lydia Maria Child.
Boston: Ticknor and Fields, 1865. 198–203.

What distinguishes the Crafts' narrative from others in the genre is its attention given to the beginnings of the couple's nineteen-year expatriation in England. From Douglass's *Narrative* to Jacobs's *Incidents in the Life of a Slave Girl*, the majority of nineteenth-century slave narratives ended with the fugitives poised to begin new chapters of their stories in the nominally free North. Since Child had edited *Incidents* and, thus, was very familiar with this literary tradition, her post–Civil War inclusion of the Crafts' English experiences seems meaningful. First, she selects this detailed account of their activities in England for a reader to be distributed among literacy programs for the newly freed slaves. This illustrates how very conscious Child must have been that ex-slaves like the Crafts (called here Mr. and Mrs. *Crafts*), whose English lives were models of industry, respectability, and good sense, represented the kind of real-life black successes whom millions of recently manumitted slaves could themselves aspire to become. It may seem initially startling that she paints William Craft as a peace-loving and civilized foil to his African brother, the King of Dahomey (Benin), who has been reduced to constant warfare with his neighbors in order to feed black bodies into the Atlantic slave trade that whites have introduced. In the context of the Reconstruction, however, William's trip to Africa is an allegory of how free and fugitive American blacks might assist their own less fortunate people in creating peaceful, pleasant communities. Child's hope for "Christian churches" and "school-houses" over Africa, and the Africans' "communication with a better class of white men," might as well be a petition for America's freedmen and freedwomen to find God, become educated, and discriminate wisely between their white allies and enemies.

※※※

In 1860, Mr. Crafts published a little book giving an account of their "Running a Thousand Miles for Freedom." They have now been living in

England fifteen years. By their united industry and good management they earned a comfortable living, and laid by a little, year after year, until they had enough to buy a small house in the village of Hammersmith, not far from the great city of London. There they keep their children at the best of schools, and pay taxes which help to support the poor in the country which protected them in their time of danger and distress.

The honesty, energy, and good sense of Mr. Crafts inspired so much respect and confidence in England, that the Quakers and other benevolent people, who wish to do good to Africa, also merchants, who want to open trade with that region, sent him out there with a valuable cargo of goods, in November, 1862. The mission he is performing is very important to the well-being of the world, as you will see by the following explanation.

Africa is four thousand miles across the Atlantic Ocean from the United States. It is inhabited by numerous tribes of black people, each tribe with a separate government. These tribes vary in degrees of intelligence and civilization; but they are generally of a peaceable and kindly disposition, unless greatly provoked by wrongs from others. Where they are safe from attack they live in little villages of huts, and raise yams, rice, and other grain for food. They weave coarse cloth from cotton, merely by means of sticks stuck in the ground, and in some places they color it with gay patterns. They make very pretty baskets and mats from grasses, and some of the tribes manufacture rude tools of iron and ornaments of gold. But a constant state of warfare has hindered the improvement of the Africans; for men have very little encouragement to build good houses, and make convenient furniture, and plant grain, if enemies are likely to come any night and burn and trample it all to the ground. These continual wars have been largely caused by the slave-trade. Formerly the African chiefs sold men into Slavery only in punishment for some crime they had committed, or to work out a debt they had failed to pay, or because they were prisoners taken in war. These customs were barbarous enough, but they were not so bad as what they were afterward taught to do by nations calling themselves Christians. In various countries of Europe and America there were white people too proud and lazy to work, but desirous to dress in the best and live on the fat of the land. They sent ships out to Africa to bring them negroes, whom they compelled to work without wages, with coarse, scanty food, and scarcely any clothing. They grew rich on the labor of these poor creatures, and spent their own time in drinking, gambling, and horse-racing.

Slave-traders, in order to supply them with as many negroes as they wanted, would steal all the men, women, and children they could catch on the coast of Africa; and would buy others from the chiefs, paying them mostly in rum and powder. This made the different tribes very desirous to go to war with each other, in order to take prisoners to sell to the slave-traders; and the more rum they drank, the more full of fight they were. This mean and cruel business has been carried on by white men four hundred years; and all that while African villages have been burned in the night, and harvests trampled, and men, women, and children carried off to hopeless Slavery in distant lands. This continual violence, and intercourse with such bad white men as the slave-traders, kept the Africans barbarous; and made them much more barbarous than they would otherwise have been. Such a state of things made it impossible for them to improve, as they would have done if the nations called Christians had sent them spelling-books and Bibles instead of rum, teachers instead of slave-traders, and tools and machinery instead of gun-powder.

Of all the African chiefs the King of Dahomey is the most powerful. He sends armed men all about the country to carry off people and sell them to Europeans and Americans. In that bad way he has grown richer than other chiefs, and more hard-hearted. Benevolent people in England have long desired to stop the ravages of the slave-trade and to teach the Africans better things. The dearth of cotton in the United States, occasioned by the Rebellion of the planters, turned the attention of English merchants in the same direction. It was accordingly agreed to send Mr. Crafts to Dahomey to open a trade, and try to convince the king that it would be more profitable to him to employ men in raising cotton than to sell them for slaves. He was well received by the King of Dahomey, who shows a disposition to be influenced by his judicious counsels. This is a great satisfaction to Mr. Crafts, desirous as he is of elevating people of his own color. Numbers who were destined to be sold into foreign Slavery are already employed in raising cotton in their native land. Wars will become less frequent; and the African tribes will gradually learn that the arts of peace are more profitable, as well as more pleasant. This will bring them into communication with a better class of white men; and I hope that, before another hundred years have passed away, there will be Christian churches all over Africa, and school-houses for the children.

Mr. Crafts sold all the goods he carried out in the first vessel, and managed the business so well that he was sent out with another cargo. He is now one of the most enterprising and respected merchants in that part of the world; and his labors produce better results than mere money, for they are the means of making men wiser and better. How much would have been lost to himself and the world if he had remained a slave in Georgia, not allowed to profit by his own industry, and forbidden to improve his mind by learning to read!

Mr. M[oncure] D[aniel] Conway, the son of a slaveholder in Virginia, but a very able and zealous friend of the colored people, recently visited England, and sent the following letter to Boston, where it was read with great interest by the numerous friends of William and Ellen Crafts:—

"London, October 29th, 1864

"A walk one pleasant morning across a green common, then through a quiet street of the village called Hammersmith, brought me to the house of an American whom I respect as much as any now in Europe; namely, William Crafts, once a slave in Georgia, then a hunted fugitive in Massachusetts, but now a respected citizen of England, and the man who is doing more to redeem Africa from her cruel superstitions than all other forces put together. He lately came home from Dahomey, the ship-load of goods that he had taken out to Africa from Liverpool having been entirely sold. The merchants who sent him are preparing another cargo for him, and he will probably leave the country this week. His theory is, that commerce is to destroy the abominations in the realm of Dahomey. He is very black, but he finds the color which was so much against him in America a leading advantage to him in Africa. Ellen, his wife, told us that she was too white to go with him. He was absent on business in Liverpool, and thus, to my regret, I missed the opportunity of seeing him. There was a pretty little girl, and three unusually handsome boys. They all inherit the light complexion and beauty of their mother. We found Mrs. Crafts busy packing her husband's trunk for his next voyage. She showed us a number of interesting things which he had brought from Africa. Among them were birds of bright plumage, a belt worn by the Amazons in war, a sword made by the Africans, breastpins, and other excellent specimens of work in metals. I remembered that years ago the sight of similar things inspired Clarkson with his strong faith in the improvability of the African race.

"William and Ellen Crafts own the house in which they live. After that brave flight of a thousand miles for freedom, after the dangers which surrounded them in Massachusetts, it did my heart good to see them enjoying their own simple but charming home, to see them thus living under their own vine and fig-tree, none daring to molest or make them afraid.
"M. D. Conway."

Mrs. Crafts has used her needle diligently to make garments for the colored people of the United States emancipated by President Lincoln's Proclamation. She has had the pleasure of hearing that her mother is among them, healthy, and still young looking for her years. As soon as arrangements can be made she will go to England to rejoin her daughter, whom she has not seen since her hazardous flight from Georgia.

I think all who read this romantic but true story will agree with me in thinking that few white people have shown as much intelligence, moral worth, and refinement of feeling as the fugitive slaves William and Ellen Crafts.

From *William and Ellen Craft: A Play in One Act,*
by Georgia Douglas Johnson. In *Negro History in Thirteen
Plays,* ed. Willis Richardson and May Miller.
Washington, D.C.: Associated Publishers, 1935. 353-76.

Georgia Douglas Johnson, the Georgia-born poet, playwright, and newspaper columnist, emigrated to Washington, D.C., in 1910 to find accolades
as a member of the Harlem Renaissance, or the New Negro movement. Her
home in northwest Washington was a lively salon for the African American
literati. Like the poet Anne Spencer's residence at 1313 Pierce Street in
Lynchburg, Johnson's household was recognized as a haven strategically
placed between the North and Deep South, where black friends and col-
leagues traveling in a segregated era could find food, a warm bed, and
thoughtful conversation. While this play, one of four of hers extant, was
very likely written for classroom use, its significance extends beyond this
purpose. Writing in her introduction to Johnson's *Selected Works* (Boston:
G.K. Hall, 1997), Claudia Tate suggests that we value this play for its "intimate moments in the lives of these runaway slaves that were effaced in abolitionist literature." In *Running,* for instance, William rarely uses the terms
of endearment such as "honey" and "dear" and the homespun reassur-
ances ("You doin fine!", "You sho learn fass") that characterize Johnson's
William. Instead, he presents his love for Ellen with rather stock descrip-
tions. It is also important to note another change: The Crafts speak in dialect in Johnson's play. This shift reminds us that, influenced by the popular
literary genres of the day, black nineteenth-century writers like the Crafts
used language as a signature of class mobility: dialect for the low, ignorant,
and lazy characters; proper English for the refined, intelligent, and aspir-
ing ones. Johnson's pairing of dialect with the noteworthy Crafts assigns a
value to such speech that, in their own time, the Crafts themselves could
not afford to do.

ELLEN
(*Going up to* WILLIAM *trembling.*)
You sho you kin git us through, William?

WILLIAM
Sho honey; ain't I been on the train time an' time agin wid young Marse, an'
can't I read and write?

ELLEN
But how kin I be like young Marse? I'm all a shakin' now.

WILLIAM
(*Soothing her.*)
All you got to do is to walk. You don't have to talk, you don't have to do a
thing but just walk along bigity like a white man. See here.
(*Shows her how to walk.*)
Try it.

ELLEN
(*Tries to walk like him.*)
Dis way?

WILLIAM
You doin fine! You see now you is supposed to be sick, you got a toothache,
you goin' to a doctor in Philadelphia, you is nearly deaf, an' yo' nigger slave
is takin' you—understand? Oh-o-o-.

ELLEN
What's wrong?

WILLIAM
Nothin' 'tall. Gimme yo' shears. I got to cut yo' hair. You see you is a
man now.

ELLEN
(*Despairingly.*)
Oh my hair!
(*She gets the scissors from the sewing basket, and brings them to him.*)

WILLIAM
(*Placing chair near table where the candle is lighted.*)
Set here.

(He goes to shutter, makes sure it is tight, walks back to Ellen, who has let down her long hair.)
I hates to cut yo' pretty hair, but . . .

ELLEN
(Resignedly.)
Anything is better than goin' down de ribber.

WILLIAM
(Takes a lock of hair to cut it when there is a sound of voices and footsteps outside of the door.)
Specks you better git behind the curtain, somebody might drop in.

ELLEN
Yes.
(Rising.)
That tale-tellin' Sam's got a way ov droppin' in here right free lak.

WILLIAM
That would be terrible! He'd be sho to git suspicious.

ELLEN
(Halting as she raises the curtain.)
If he do drap in whut we goin' to say? How we goin' to git him out?

WILLIAM
Oh, I'll say you sick—got a headache or something or other, an' gone to bed. I'll git a few horseredish leaves out of the garden an' lay one or two on de table to make it look natul like.

ELLEN
(Entering into the spirit.)
Yes, an' I'll put de coffee pot on some coals an' you kin say you makin' me some coffee to he'p me.

WILLIAM
You sho learn fass. You'se reel smart. I knows you'se goin' to make this trip perfect.

ELLEN
(Beaming, moves toward the table as WILLIAM *moves toward the door.)*
Hurry William!

SUGGESTIONS FOR FURTHER READING

Compiled by Barbara McCaskill

Andrews, William L. *To Tell a Free Story: The First Century of Afro-American Autobiography, 1760–1865.* Urbana: University of Illinois Press, 1986.

Blackett, Richard J. M. *Building an Antislavery Wall: Black Americans in the Atlantic Abolitionist Movement, 1830–1860.* Baton Rouge: Louisiana State University Press, 1983.

———. "The Odyssey of William and Ellen Craft." In *Beating against the Barriers: Biographical Essays in Nineteenth-Century Afro-American History.* Baton Rouge: Louisiana State University Press, 1972.

———. "'To Reach the People with Abolition Doctrines': The Antislavery Press and the American Civil War." *Atlanta History: A Journal of Georgia and the South* 42:1–2 (spring–summer 1998): 35–44.

Blassingame, John W. *The Slave Community: Plantation Life in the Antebellum South.* New York: Oxford University Press, 1972.

———, ed. *Slave Testimony: Two Centuries of Letters, Speeches, Interviews, and Autobiographies.* Baton Rouge: Louisiana State University Press, 1977.

Blockson, Charles L. *The Underground Railroad: First-Person Narratives of Escape to Freedom in the North.* New York: Prentice-Hall, 1987.

Brown, Josephine. *Biography of an American Bondman, by His Daughter.* In *Two Biographies by African-American Women.* New York: Oxford University Press, 1991. 3–104.

Brown, William Wells. *Clotel; or, The President's Daughter: A Narrative of Slave Life in the United States.* London: Partridge and Oakey, 1853.

———. *The Travels of William Wells Brown, Including Narrative of William Wells Brown, a Fugitive Slave and the American Fugitive in Europe. Sketches of People and Places Abroad. The Travels of William Wells Brown,* edited by Paul Jefferson. New York: Markus Weiner Publishing, 1991. 71–235.

———. *Three Years in Europe; Or, Places I Have Seen and People I Have Met.* London: Charles Gilpin, 1852.

Burkett, Randall K., et al., eds. *Black Biography, 1790–1950: A Cumulative Index.* Alexandria, Va.: Chadwyck-Healey, 1991.

Campbell, Edward D. C., with Kym S. Rice, eds. *Before Freedom Came: African-American Life in the Antebellum South.* Richmond: The Museum of the Confederacy and the University Press of Virginia, 1991. 100–121.

Child, Lydia Maria. *The Freedmen's Book.* Boston: Ticknor and Fields, 1865.

———. *The Stars and Stripes: A Melo-Drama.* In *The Liberty Bell.* Boston: Prentiss, Sawyer, 1858. 122–85.

Clift-Pellow, Arlene. "Ellen Craft." In *Epic Lives: One Hundred Black Women Who Made a Difference,* edited by Jessie Carney Smith. Detroit: Visible Ink Press, 1993. 135–40.

"A Daring Flight through the South." *African American Voices of Triumph.* Vol. 1, *Perseverance.* Alexandria, Va.: Time-Life Books, 1993. 58–59.

Davis, Charles T., and Henry Louis Gates Jr., eds. *The Slave's Narrative.* New York: Oxford University Press, 1985.

Farrison, William Edward. *William Wells Brown, Author and Reformer.* Chicago: University of Chicago Press, 1969.

Foster, Frances Smith. *Witnessing Slavery: The Development of the Ante-Bellum Slave Narratives.* Westport, Conn.: Greenwood Press, 1979.

Freedman, Florence B. *Two Tickets for Freedom: The True Story of Ellen and William Craft, Fugitive Slaves.* New York: Peter Bedrick Books, 1971.

Frothingham, Octavius Brooks. *Theodore Parker: A Biography.* Boston: James R. Osgood and Company, 1874.

Garber, Marjorie. "Passing to Freedom: The Art of the Crafts." In *Vested Interests: Cross-Dressing and Cultural Anxiety.* New York: Routledge, 1992. 282–85.

Horton, James Oliver, and Lois E. Horton. *Black Bostonians: Family Life and Community Struggle in the Antebellum North.* New York: Holmes and Meier, 1979.

Jacobs, Donald M., ed. *Courage and Conscience: Black and White Abolitionists in Boston.* Bloomington: Indiana University Press for the Boston Athenaeum, 1993.

Karcher, Carolyn L. *The First Woman of the Republic: A Cultural Biography of Lydia Maria Child.* Durham, N.C.: Duke University Press, 1994.

Loewenberg, Bert James, and Ruth Bogin, eds. *Black Women in Nineteenth-*

Century American Life: Their Words, Their Thoughts, Their Feelings.
University Park: Pennsylvania State University Press, 1976.

McCaskill, Barbara. "A Stamp on the Envelope Upside Down Means Love." In *Multicultural Literature and Literacies: Making Space for Difference,* edited by Suzanne Miller and Barbara McCaskill. Albany: State University of New York Press, 1993. 77–102.

———. "'Trust No Man!' But What about a Woman?: Ellen Craft and a Genealogical Model for Teaching Douglass' *Narrative.*" In *Approaches to Teaching the Narrative of the Life of Frederick Douglass,* edited by James C. Hall. New York: Modern Language Association, forthcoming.

———. "'Yours Very Truly': Ellen Craft—The Fugitive as Text and Artifact." *African American Review* 28:4 (winter 1994): 509–29.

Meltzer, Milton, and Patricia G. Holland, eds. *Lydia Maria Child: Selected Letters 1817–1880.* Amherst: University of Massachusetts Press, 1982.

Morton, Patricia D., ed. *Discovering the Women in Slavery: Emancipating Perspectives on the American Past.* Athens: The University of Georgia Press, 1996.

Nelson, Dana D. "William and Ellen Craft." In *The Oxford Companion to African-American Literature,* edited by William L. Andrews, Frances Smith Foster, and Trudier Harris. New York: Oxford University Press, 1997. 182.

Quarles, Benjamin. *Black Abolitionists.* New York: Oxford University Press, 1969.

Ripley, C. Peter, et al., eds. *The Black Abolitionist Papers.* 5 vols. Chapel Hill: University of North Carolina Press, 1985.

Sekora, John, and Darwin T. Turner, eds. *The Art of Slave Narrative: Original Essays in Criticism and Theory.* Macomb: Western Illinois University Press, 1982.

"Singular Escapes from Slavery." In *Five Hundred Thousand Strokes for Freedom, A Series of Anti-Slavery Tracts, of which Half a Million are Now First Issued by the Friends of the Negro.* Leeds Anti-Slavery Series, No. 35. 1853. Reprint, Miami: Mnemosyne, 1969. 4–8.

Starling, Marion Wilson. *The Slave Narrative: Its Place in American History.* 2d ed. Washington, D.C.: Howard University Press, 1988.

Sterling, Dorothy. "Ellen Craft: The Valiant Journey." *Black Foremothers: Three Lives.* 2d ed. Old Westbury, N.Y.: Feminist Press, 1988. 3–59.

———, ed. *We Are Your Sisters: Black Women in the Nineteenth Century*. New York: Norton, 1984.

Still, William. *The Underground Rail Road: A Record of Facts, Authentic Narratives, Letters, &c., Narrating the Hardships, Hair-Breadth Escapes, and Death Struggles of the Slaves in Their Efforts for Freedom, As Related by Themselves and Others or Witnessed by the Author: Together with Sketches of Some of the Largest Stockholders and Most Liberal Aiders and Advisers of the Road*. Philadelphia: Porter and Coates, 1872.

Von Frank, Albert J. *The Trials of Anthony Burns: Freedom and Slavery in Emerson's Boston*. Cambridge, Mass.: Harvard University Press, 1998.

Weiss, John. *Life and Correspondence of Theodore Parker*. Vol. 2. New York: D. Appleton and Company, 1864.

White, Deborah Gray. *Ar'n't I a Woman?: Female Slaves in the Plantation South*. New York: W. W. Norton, 1985.

Woodson, Carter G., ed. *The Mind of the Negro as Reflected in Letters Written during the Crisis, 1800–1860*. Washington, D.C.: Association for the Study of Negro Life and History, 1926.

Yee, Shirley J. *Black Women Abolitionists: A Study in Activism, 1828–1860*. Knoxville: The University of Tennessee Press, 1992.

Yellin, Jean Fagan. "Hiram Powers's *The Greek Slave*." In *Women and Sisters: The Antislavery Feminists in American Culture*. New Haven: Yale University Press, 1989. 99–124.

———. *The Intricate Knot: Black Figures in American Literature, 1776–1863*. New York: New York University Press, 1972.

CPSIA information can be obtained at www.ICGtesting.com
Printed in the USA
LVOW08s0636110813

347217LV00005B/13/P